Praise for **JESUS IS** _____.

"Judah Smith is a unique gift to my generation. In *Jesus Is* _____, he will motivate you to let go of your preconceived, limited view of Jesus so you can embrace who He really is in our lives—more real and relevant than we have ever imagined."

—STEVEN FURTICK, LEAD PASTOR, ELEVATION CHURCH AND
AUTHOR OF THE *NEW YORK TIMES* BESTSELLER *GREATER*

"Perhaps the most daunting and humbling task we have as Christians is to finish the sentence 'Jesus is . . . .' As many of us saved by His grace are aware, He is King. He is Lord. He is salvation. But to many in our world, He is most prominently . . . misunderstood. There is not another human being on earth whom I know personally, who could tackle a book subject like this as well as Judah Smith. To Judah, Jesus is everything. And from that platform he writes this book. I eagerly await its impact in my city, New York City, and beyond . . . it's overdue."

—CARL LENTZ, LEAD PASTOR,
HILLSONG CHURCH, NEW YORK CITY

"Every once in a while a book is written that does not only contain a powerful message but the author is a living embodiment of the message thus making the book all the more life changing! The book you are holding in your hands is one of those. As you read through this book you will discover that Jesus is not at all like you thought and so much more than you imagined."

—CHRISTINE CAINE, FOUNDER
OF THE A21 CAMPAIGN

"This book gives any reader—regardless of where they are in their faith walk—the inspiration to redefine and reignite a new relationship with Jesus."

—TOMMY BARNETT, SENIOR PASTOR, PHOENIX FIRST
AND FOUNDER OF THE LOS ANGELES DREAM CENTER

"I am honoured that Judah considers me his Pastor. His understanding of who Christ is, of who he is in Christ, and his passion to see people know Jesus is contagious and well beyond his years. This is his life message—to discover the person of Christ and communicate the truth of who Jesus is. We may never know the fullness of the Son of Man this side of eternity and words may fail when we try to uncover who Jesus Is ____, but Judah's revelation in this book will set you on a journey of falling even more in love with the unending characteristics of the greatest man who ever lived."

—BRIAN HOUSTON, SENIOR PASTOR, HILLSONG CHURCH

"Who is Jesus to you? Finding the answer to this question will change your life forever. Judah Smith is on a mission to share the truth about Jesus, and if you are searching to know more, you will find it in *Jesus Is ____*."

—CRAIG GROESCHEL, SENIOR PASTOR OF
LIFECHURCH.TV AND AUTHOR OF *SOUL DETOX:
CLEAN LIVING IN A CONTAMINATED WORLD*

"I love this book because Judah Smith nails the big question of human existence. Everything else is minor compared to deciding who Jesus is, and what that means in our lives. It's that simple."

—MILES MCPHERSON, PASTOR, SPEAKER, AND
AUTHOR OF *GOD IN THE MIRROR: DISCOVERING
WHO YOU WERE CREATED TO BE*

"My good friend Judah Smith is the real deal, and might be the best communicator on the planet. This game-changing book will inspire, challenge, and jolt you toward the person of Jesus, reminding us that He in fact is true life. Judah's passion for people and spreading the gospel is evident throughout his writing, and I know *Jesus Is* ___ will be a message and movement that will transform the lives of many, and has already changed me."

—BRAD LOMENICK, PRESIDENT OF CATALYST
AND AUTHOR OF *THE CATALYST LEADER*

"For so many of us, our concept of Jesus comes from culture and tradition, not what the Bible actually says. With compelling passion and creativity, Judah helps us look through the clutter of stereotypes and connects us to who Jesus really is. The truths in this book will change your life!"

—CHRIS HODGES, SENIOR PASTOR, CHURCH OF
THE HIGHLANDS AND AUTHOR OF *FRESH AIR*

"If you truly grasp the concept of this book it will change your life. We all have questions about our faith. Judah has a gift of navigating through all the religious rhetoric and sheds light on who God is, in a way I've never seen before. At the end of this book I guarantee you will feel loved by your Creator."

—JASON KENNEDY, E! NEWS CORRESPONDENT

"Judah Smith is one of the best communicators I have ever heard. He is authentic, passionate, humorous, and wise beyond his years. This book will inspire you and make you laugh at the same time. It will also challenge and encourage you. As always, with Judah it is all about Jesus."

—NICKY GUMBEL, VICAR OF HOLY TRINITY
BROMPTON AND PIONEER OF THE ALPHA COURSE

"The discussion of who Jesus would be began thousands of years before he was even born. Today, the discussion (and along with it, the confusion) continues. But in *Jesus Is ____*, my friend Judah Smith breaks down barriers and clears up confusion about the most influential personality the world has ever known. Whether you know, you think you know, or you have no concept who Jesus is, this book is a must-read!"

—ED YOUNG, SENIOR PASTOR, FELLOWSHIP CHURCH
AND AUTHOR OF *OUTRAGEOUS, CONTAGIOUS JOY*

"Judah Smith explains in such a clear and thoughtful manner who Jesus Christ is and what he means to our lives. In his book *Jesus Is ____*, Judah presents an elaborate guide to the life of Christ, his sacrifice to save mankind, and the power of His grace. The love of Christ is such a revolutionary gift at work all around us. Judah Smith clearly has a servant's heart and an extensive understanding of Christ's nature. Jesus is our savior, our friend, our mentor, and our purpose in all things. Jesus Christ is alive, and this book paints that reality in beautiful and striking language."

—PASTOR MATTHEW BARNETT, COFOUNDER
OF THE LOS ANGELES DREAM CENTER

"Judah, through explaining who Jesus is, teaches how *we* as forgiven people have the supernatural strength to forgive others and live a blessed life of freedom. Why let your past failures hold you back when Jesus has already paid for them? Judah, as a positive force, teaches what he knows, loves, and believes in . . . Jesus. As he'll often say 'I'm a Jesus guy.'"

—RYAN GOOD, STYLIST FOR JUSTIN BIEBER
AND PRODUCER OF TV SHOW *PUNK'D*

JUDAH SMITH

JESUS IS _____.

FIND A
NEW WAY
TO BE
HUMAN

THOMAS NELSON
Since 1798

NASHVILLE DALLAS MEXICO CITY RIO DE JANEIRO

Published in Nashville, Tennessee, by Thomas Nelson. Thomas Nelson is a registered trademark of Thomas Nelson, Inc.

Published in association with the literary agency of Fedd & Company, Inc., P.O. Box 341973, Austin, TX 78734.

Thomas Nelson, Inc., titles may be purchased in bulk for educational, business, fund-raising, or sales promotional use. For information, please e-mail SpecialMarkets@ThomasNelson.com.

Library of Congress Cataloging-in-Publication Data

Smith, Judah.
 Jesus is : find a new way to be human / Judah Smith.
   p. cm.
 Includes bibliographical references.
 ISBN 978-1-4002-0475-5
 1. Jesus Christ--Person and offices. I. Title.
 BT203.S615 2013
 232--dc23

                    2012035782

Printed in the United States of America

13 14 15 16 17 QG 6 5 4 3 2 1

This book is dedicated to the community I have been privileged to be a part of since I was 13, the City Church. This is our journey.

Contents

CONTENTS

Foreword

by Bubba Watson

Sometimes God takes your life for some crazy twists and turns.

When I first heard the name Judah Smith, my dad was just weeks away from being called home to heaven. My trainer, Andrew Fischer, started talking about this great young pastor and encouraged me to listen to him online. He said his name was Judah Smith from Seattle.

A few days later I was checking Twitter, and I noticed a pastor from Seattle named Judah Smith was following me. I wrote and told him that my trainer listened to him online, and we started swapping notes across Twitter over the next several weeks.

Then my dad passed away. He'd been battling cancer for a while, but nothing prepares you for your dad dying—even when you know it's coming. I was closer to my dad than to just about anyone else. He was my coach on and off the course. It was a rough time.

Judah was quick to send me some inspiring messages from the Bible. It was a heartfelt gesture and really meant the world to me at that moment. I had no idea at the time that Judah was going through the very same thing. His dad was fighting cancer too. Just two months after my dad passed his dad was called to heaven as well.

Everything from that time is very vivid. I remember it like it was yesterday. I messaged Judah on Twitter to get his phone number. I called him five days after his dad's death and asked if he wanted to come down to my house to play golf. What can I say? Judah's a pastor; he shared Bible verses. I'm a golfer; I shared the green. Judah and his family packed their bags and headed down to Scottsdale.

Judah said he was a .7 handicap at golf, but he shot high 80s that first day we played golf—and not much better after that.

Like I said, God takes you for some crazy twist and turns. The only way you can explain my friendship with Judah is God's plan. Judah has made me stronger in my walk with Christ. He has been a great role model in all parts of life. Judah has helped me be more consistent in seeking God's will and trusting the Lord daily. As our friendship has grown, he has taught me to be a better husband, better dad, better friend, better listener, everything—except maybe a better golfer!

How does he do it? He just shares Jesus. That's what gets Judah started and keeps him going. He wants to help people meet Jesus and become more like Jesus.

I hope *Jesus Is* _____ will help you do exactly that. It's a simple message, but it's the kind of message every one of us needs to hear.

Introduction

I'm thirty-three years old, and I was born and raised in the Pacific Northwest, which means I'm addicted to coffee and complaining about the weather. I'm a husband, a father of three, and an okay golfer. I'm also a pastor.

That last bit often makes people feel awkward. They try not to swear around me, which mostly makes me laugh. They think I can't relate to them. A pastor, of course, doesn't swear, have impure thoughts, yell at his kids, watch porn, get drunk, do drugs, or cheat on his wife or taxes. He also judges everyone he sees, doesn't have any fun, tries not to smile, and only has sex because it's a necessary evil in order to perpetuate the species.

Those are stereotypes, of course. Some are true and some are not. But none of them tell the whole story about what it means to be a pastor, a Christian, or even a good person.

Over the last few years, I've been on a journey that has challenged stereotypes—of myself, of sin and sinners, of Jesus himself. It's hard to describe the depth of the transformation

I've experienced, but I do know this: I'll never be the same again.

Christianity is not about not swearing. It's not about not having impure thoughts. Really, it's not about not at all.

Christianity is about Jesus.

The Campaign

About three years ago, soon after becoming lead pastor, I sat down with the media team at my church and told them I wanted to launch a marketing campaign in our city. My goal: to get Jesus on the mind of Seattle.

I didn't want to promote our church. I didn't want to promote a doctrine. I just wanted people to think more about Jesus.

Out of that little meeting came the "Jesus Is ____" campaign. Our marketing consisted of billboards, bus signs, Facebook ads, bumper magnets (not stickers—people love their cars), and a website, jesus-is.org, where people could fill in the blank themselves. We also organized hundreds of what we called "Jesus Is ____ Projects": social outreach events organized by people in our church who cleaned up parks, volunteered at schools, and did other community service projects.

The premise of the campaign was simply to get people thinking about Jesus. We felt that indifference was our greatest enemy. If we could get people to think about Jesus, we reasoned, Jesus was more than able to reveal himself to them.

The response was overwhelming. People have visited

different pages on our website over one and a half million times. Seventy-five thousand people and counting have submitted answers to the blank. The campaign has been mentioned on atheist websites, porn websites, and church websites. Hackers have targeted it multiple times.

Apparently, Jesus gets a reaction out of people.

The answers people submit are incredibly moving. Perusing the website provides a fascinating commentary on our culture's concept of Jesus. Many submissions, of course, are pro-Jesus. Others are simply funny. Some are bizarre. Many are blatantly anti-Jesus: they are blasphemous, hateful, even perverse.

Within months of launching the campaign, we realized something. Jesus Is ——— was more than a clever campaign or a marketing mantra. It was the mission of our church.

A giant chalkboard in our church lobby now reads, "Our mission: to show you who Jesus is." Underneath, hundreds of handwritten definitions appear each week as people in our church celebrate who Jesus is to them.

I can't think of a better mission in life. I'll probably write more books, but I doubt I will ever write one as important as this. At the same time, this book barely scratches the surface of who Jesus is. Discovering the depths of his love has become my obsession, my passion, and my delight.

The Bible

I am a Bible person. I don't believe my brain has been function-ing long enough to figure out the meaning of life, but the Bible is an amazing, divine, supernatural book that shows us the plan of God. It gives us proper perspective in life. I believe that God used humans to write it, but he guided what they wrote, and everything in it is accurate.

It doesn't bother me if you don't believe that, so I hope it doesn't bother you that I do believe it. Actually, I think this book makes sense even if you don't believe it, so it would be great if you approached it with an open mind. None of us has the whole truth, including me, but we can learn from each other.

The Bible is meant to be down-to-earth. It was written for real people facing real issues. So when I preach and write, I often retell Bible narratives in my own words. It's not a new translation; it's a paraphrase, usually with a good dose of humor thrown in. Sometimes I crack myself up; but laughter is biblical, so I feel almost holy laughing at my own jokes.

My Sticky-Note Brain

You'll discover this soon enough, so I might as well spell it out. I am not a very linear person.

That will delight some of you and frustrate others. I have the attention span of a five-year-old, which is actually fine by me, because five-year-olds enjoy life a heck of a lot more than most adults.

Some of you have brains filled with filing cabinets, all lined up in neat rows. Everything is indexed and alphabetized. You quantify and qualify and calculate your lives, and that's awesome. God bless you.

The walls of my brain are covered with sticky notes. And the sticky notes are filled with scribbles. And the scribbles are highlighted in multiple neon colors. So if I jump around a bit in this book, now you know why. Pray for me.

A Final Note

I would not be who I am without the influence of my dad, Wendell Smith. He passed away from cancer in December 2010, and I miss him every day. He was my mentor, my friend, and my hero.

He and my mom, Gini, founded the City Church in 1992. They pastored for seventeen years before turning the church over to my wife, Chelsea, and me in 2009. My dad's faith, generosity, and love were beyond equal.

My father showed me who Jesus is. He started me on a journey of delight and discovery that continues each day.

My prayer is that as you read this book, you also would see Jesus for who he really is. And when you do, he will be irresistible.

JESUS IS your friend.

ONE

Superbad or Sortabad

"If God can help so-and-so, he can help *anyone!*"

I've heard myself say it a few times. "So-and-so" is always a reference to skilled sinners, famous for their proficiency in wrongdoing. They are awesome at sin, they sin a lot, and they enjoy their sin.

"Did you hear? That actress got another divorce. That's five failed marriages and this marriage only lasted three months. Man, if God could get her straightened out, he could help anybody!"

"That leader calls himself a Christian, but can you believe what he was involved in? He should be ashamed of himself. If God can help him, he can help anybody!"

Let's be honest. Mostly good people like to look down on mostly bad people. We enjoy the feelings of condescending pity or self-righteous outrage. We gleefully hold up notorious evildoers as marvels of depravity, examples of just how bad people can get. Then we finish off our lattes, load our

2.2 children into our almost-paid-off SUVs, and head off to contribute to society.

Notice how I just included myself in the "mostly good" category. I didn't think about it. I just did it.

That's what bothers me the most.

The Badness Scale

The problem with the "if God can save . . ." statement is that it implies a rating system for sins. It's an unspoken, often culture-driven, and arbitrary badness scale (or goodness scale, depending on whether we are rating others or ourselves).

On our scale, we label small sins, medium-small sins, medium sins, medium-large sins, large sins, extra-large sins, and supersized sins. If we see someone with small to medium sins, we think, *He's a pretty good person. He's fairly sound and engaged morally. He's obviously close to Jesus. It won't be hard for God to get a hold of him.*

Then we see someone with medium to large sins, and we get more nervous. *We really have to pray for her. Her life is going downhill fast. God is going to have to get her attention the hard way. She really needs to work on fixing herself so she can get closer to God.*

When we come across a supersize sinner, someone who commits the big sins, we just shake our heads in hyper-pious pity.

Nowhere in the Bible, however, do we find God distinguishing between levels of sin. God doesn't share our rating system. To him, all sin is equally evil, and all sinners are equally lovable. Obviously sins have different consequences: some will get you incarcerated or your face punched in, while others won't even be noticed. But God just calls sin, *sin*.

Zacchaeus the Gangster

Jesus didn't have a rating system for sin, either. He was willing to accept anyone, to love anyone. Nowhere is this more evident than in the story of Zacchaeus the tax collector.

I should mention up front that when I read Bible stories, all the main characters have accents. That's just how my mind works. Concentration has never been my strong suit, and I suspect the accents are a desperate ploy sponsored by my brain to keep me focused.

Zacchaeus, in my mind, was a bit of a gangster. If you can't read his dialogue with a bit of swagger, you and I are not going to connect very well for the next few pages. You may need to listen to a few hip-hop albums and try again.

In case you aren't familiar with the story, Zacchaeus was a tax collector. Actually, he was a chief tax collector. He was also really short. That's important.

Here's the story, straight from the Bible:

Jesus entered Jericho and made his way through the town. There was a man there named Zacchaeus. He was the chief tax collector in the region, and he had become very rich. He tried to get a look at Jesus, but he was too short to see over the crowd. So he ran ahead and climbed a sycamore-fig tree beside the road, for Jesus was going to pass that way.

When Jesus came by, he looked up at Zacchaeus and called him by name. "Zacchaeus!" he said. "Quick, come down! I must be a guest in your home today."

Zacchaeus quickly climbed down and took Jesus to his house in great excitement and joy. But the people were displeased. "He has gone to be the guest of a notorious sinner," they grumbled.

Meanwhile, Zacchaeus stood before the Lord and said, "I will give half my wealth to the poor, Lord, and if I have cheated people on their taxes, I will give them back four times as much!"

Jesus responded, "Salvation has come to this home today, for this man has shown himself to be a true son of Abraham. For the Son of Man came to seek and save those who are lost." (Luke 19:1–10)

Interesting backstory: Israelites of Jesus's day looked at tax collectors as thieves and pimps. Tax collectors were Jews who worked for the Roman government, which ruled Israel at the time. Their job was to collect taxes from their own people and hand the money over to the hated foreign power. Their own income came from whatever they could get out of people after they met Rome's quota. So Zacchaeus and his fellow tax-collecting traitors would make up tax amounts on the fly. Zacchaeus was a professional cheat, an embezzler. He took money from little old ladies. He was a thief.

I think Zacchaeus was up on pop culture, by the way. I think he liked making appearances; he liked being in on the action. When they rolled out the red carpet and the cameras showed up, Zacchaeus was going to be there, a lady on each arm, looking over his sunglasses at the crew from TMZ. "Hey y'all." When he gave press conferences, he talked about himself in the third person.

Zacchaeus was a short guy, but don't be deceived by his stature. He had a lot of money. At some point, years before, he had been recruited by the Romans. He was probably a bit of a prodigy. He would have started out as an assistant to a tax collector. After proving his worth, he would have been promoted to tax collector. Ultimately, when we find him in this story, he has become the chief tax collector. He probably oversees an entire tax district and a gang of mini tax collectors who give him a cut of their take.

This makes Zacchaeus a major reject. He is infamous, legendary, notorious. How long has he been doing this? Five years? Longer than that—he's a chief tax collector. Ten years? Twenty?

I don't think he minds being hated. In fact, I think he's loving life. He's up in his big house overlooking the city, lounging in his infinity pool, with servants fanning him and dropping grapes in his mouth.

Everybody fears him now. Sure, they hate him—but at least they respect him. Back in elementary school, nobody picked the short guy. But now, they're afraid of the little man. Zacchaeus is the big guy on the block.

Rumor was, Jesus might be the promised Messiah. Zacchaeus had grown up in the Jewish culture, and he would have been familiar with the prophecies. No doubt he had heard that one day there would come a Messiah. Now Jesus is coming through town, and Zacchaeus says, "I'm gonna check this guy out. He's getting a lot of followers; a lot of guys are talking about him. I'm curious."

I doubt Zacchaeus was thinking, *Man, I sure hope Jesus saves me.* Saves him from what? His big house? All the ladies who love him?

No, he just wanted to check out the popular guy. Zacchaeus was all about status. You don't become a tax collector and then a chief tax collector and not like money and status. He was famous in a negative sense, but famous nonetheless.

Jesus starts strolling through. People are lining the streets, trying to catch a glimpse of him, and Zacchaeus realizes he can't see over the crowd. *This is jacked up,* he says to himself. *I'm not gonna be able to see this dude.*

Zacchaeus is an innovative guy who is used to getting his way. So he hitches up his blinged-out robe and runs ahead, gold chains clanking, and climbs a sycamore tree.

Sure enough, he can see the dust cloud and all the people clumped around Jesus. You'd think he was Justin Bieber or something. He's rolling down the street, and suddenly—Zacchaeus can't believe his luck—he stops right next to the little man's tree.

This is dope, he's thinking. *I can check this guy out from up here; maybe listen in on what he's got to say.*

Then, to Zacchaeus's surprise, Jesus looks up at him. He calls him by name. "Zacchaeus."

"Whaaaa? How do you know me? I don't know you. Who told you about me?"

They say the sweetest sound to a human being's ears is the sound of his or her own name. God calls this rejected, hardened, selfish man by his name: "Zacchaeus, hurry down! I'm heading over to your house—right now."

"You are? Uh, okay. Yeah."

Zacchaeus is relishing the moment. All the upstanding religious Jews want a minute with Jesus, a nod, a handshake. Yet now, the chief tax collector—the biggest bad guy around—gets a personal invitation. I think he's looking at everyone saying, "Whassup now, y'all?" He sends word to all his cronies and tax collector minions to come over and meet this Jesus. This is his moment in the limelight.

"I'm Changing Everything"

But that afternoon, something unexpected and unexplainable began to happen in Zacchaeus's heart. How long did he have an audience with the living God? Two hours? Four hours? We don't know. What did they talk about? We can only guess.

We can assume that they ate a meal together and Jesus probably listened a lot. Zacchaeus must have thought, *Nobody listens to me, except for a few guys who work for me. But this guy cares. He listens. He gets it.*

I can imagine Zacchaeus looking into the most compassionate eyes he's ever seen and thinking, *Does Jesus know who I am? Does he know who is around my dinner table? Does he know what we do for a living? Does he know what paid for his fish? Does he know how I paid for this house? He must . . . but he doesn't reject me.*

After a few hours with Jesus, Zacchaeus can't contain himself any longer. Abruptly, he stands up, seemingly overwhelmed with who this Jesus is. In front of family, peers, and employees, he blurts out, "I'm changing everything!"

What?

"I'm changing everything, Jesus. I'm gonna start giving my money away. In fact, anyone I've ever cheated, I'm gonna give them back four times what I stole."

The callous, money-hungry mob boss is about to go broke, and he doesn't even care. A moment with Jesus changed everything.

I wonder what Jesus said in one short afternoon that changed a lifelong taker into a lavish giver. But that's not the point of this passage. I think the Bible skips over what they talked about because we'd try to turn it into a recipe or a program. It wasn't what Zacchaeus talked about—it was the person he talked about it with. It was about being with Jesus.

What changed Zacchaeus? Biblical principle? Personal devotion? Religious duty and deeds? No—just a few moments with God in the flesh. We don't even have a record of anyone telling Zacchaeus he needed to repent or give the money back. But something came over this man when he encountered Jesus.

Hurry Down

The truth is, I am Zacchaeus. I may not be short in stature, but I'm short spiritually, in my own ability and my own capacity. Even if I want to get to Jesus, even if I want to see Jesus, I can't see past myself. I can't see past my sin, past my distractions, past my ego.

How do we try to reach Jesus? We run faster and we climb proverbial trees of religious actions. We think, *I'll get to Jesus. I'll impress Jesus with who I am.*

I believe most people have a sense of inadequacy and failure deep within themselves. No matter how hard they try or what they accomplish, they know they are in a dark place. They are short in a spiritual sense. They have sinned and come short of God's glorious standard. So they think, *I'll run faster, I'll run ahead, I'll find a tree and climb it, and I'll get God's attention.*

As if your running and your climbing is what gets God's attention!

That's not what saved Zacchaeus. It was God's mercy. It was God's grace. It was God's initiative.

We think God stops and takes notice of us because he sees us up in our cute sycamore trees. We think it is because we are so good. "See, I got God to notice. You see me? It's because I pray so loud, because I pray so much, because I attend church."

But that's not why Jesus stopped that day. He stopped of his own choosing. He stopped because he's gracious and he's good. He stopped because he knew Zacchaeus by name, just as he knows me and knows you.

Jesus told Zacchaeus to hurry, and he tells us the same thing. "Hurry down from religion. Hurry down from traditions. Quit trying to pick yourself up. Only my grace can save you. Come down, and come now. Don't spend another moment or another day trusting yourself. I need to be with you today."

While Zacchaeus spoke, Jesus must have been smiling to himself. But now he makes an announcement of his own. "Today, salvation has come to this house. Zacchaeus is a son of Abraham, a true Jew."

Zacchaeus is stunned. He is the quintessential traitor, the bad guy, the antithesis of a good Jew. For as long as he can remember, he's been on the outside looking in. Now he's on the inside? Now he's a good guy?

I wish I could have seen the look on his friends' faces. *If there's hope for Zacchaeus, there must be hope for me too!*

Then Jesus summed up his life mission: "I'm here to find and help lost people. That's why I've come."

The Pharisees thought the Messiah was only coming for the chosen few, for the sanctified few, for the religious few. But Jesus said over and over that he came for the broken, the bad, the addicted, the bound, the deceived, the lost, the hurting.

Sometimes we are a lot like Zacchaeus. We've been at this sin thing for a long time. We have problems, weaknesses, and propensities toward doing wrong. We've gotten a little scarred and numb to the whole thing—maybe even outright cynical. We are helpless, hopeless. *Even Jesus couldn't set me free*, we think. After all, we've tried as hard as we can and nothing has changed. He wouldn't see anything worth saving in us anyway.

Maybe it's a secret sin: an affair eight years ago that not even your spouse knows about. Maybe it's something that controls your life, like alcoholism or some other addiction. People have told you you'll never change, and you're starting to believe them.

Jesus is not your accuser. He's not your prosecutor. He's not your judge. He's your friend and your rescuer. Like Zacchaeus, just spend time with Jesus. Don't hide from him in shame or reject him in self-righteousness. Don't allow the opinions of other people to shape your concept of him. Get to know him for yourself, and let the goodness of God change you from the inside out.

TWO

Dark Side

Zacchaeus wasn't the only tax collector to have his world rocked by Jesus. There was also Matthew. Matthew was one of Jesus's disciples, and the book he wrote describes many key events in the three-plus years of Jesus's ministry.

Matthew's first encounter with Jesus reveals that when it comes to sinners, God has two categories. Just two. Matthew 9:9–13 says,

> As Jesus was walking along, he saw a man named Matthew sitting at his tax collector's booth. "Follow me and be my disciple," Jesus said to him. So Matthew got up and followed him.
>
> Later, Matthew invited Jesus and his disciples to his home as dinner guests, along with many tax collectors and other disreputable sinners. But when the Pharisees saw this, they asked his disciples, "Why does your teacher eat with such scum?"

When Jesus heard this, he said, "Healthy people don't need a doctor—sick people do." Then he added, "Now go and learn the meaning of this Scripture: 'I want you to show mercy, not offer sacrifices.' For I have come to call not those who think they are righteous, but those who know they are sinners."

Two Kinds of Sinners

Like Zacchaeus, Matthew was a tax collector. Everywhere he went, he was hated, feared, and rejected. Until he met Jesus. Matthew never forgot the inexplicable willingness of this man to look past his occupation and to see him as a person.

In Jesus's conversation with Matthew, he lumps all of humanity into two groups: people who *think* they are righteous and people who *know* they are sinners.

That's it. No sliding scale, no grading on the curve, no relative goodness or subjective labels. We either pretend we don't need him or we acknowledge we do.

The common denominator is that we all need help. The catch is that we don't all admit it. Rather than realizing everyone is in this together, that we are all in need of help, we often prop up our self-esteem by looking at people who do supposedly worse things than us.

We need to abandon our scale and adopt God's because our misguided labels keep us from the right kind of interaction with people. We assume we know where they are on the rating scale, and we assume we know whether they are ready or not to hear about Jesus and give their lives to God.

In reality, for many people, the greatest hindrance to receiving the grace of God is not their scandalous sins—it's their empty good deeds.

It's obvious some people have problems. But for the man who lives in his two-story home on a quiet cul-de-sac, keeps his lawn manicured and his cars washed, stays faithful to his wife, works hard at his job, pays his bills, and never cheats on his taxes—for that model citizen, it's not so obvious. He might compare his goodness to others' badness and think, *I'm a morally sound person. I'm doing pretty well. I don't need help.*

Our superficial labeling system also guarantees that we will never find freedom ourselves. It takes courage and humility to recognize we are as messed up as the drug addict next door, and many of us never get that honest with ourselves. If we can't be honest with ourselves, we'll never be honest with God. We'll continue to whitewash our dark sides and flaunt our good deeds, and nothing will ever change.

"Hi. I Hate You."

Jesus befriended sinners like Zacchaeus and Matthew; and the Pharisees especially couldn't handle that. Pharisees were the spiritual teachers of the day. They were experts in Jewish religious law—a set of hundreds of man-made rules that attempted to apply the Ten Commandments to everyday life. They had regulations for everything from washing hands to tying loads onto camels.

When we find Pharisees in the Bible, they are usually doing one thing: pointing out sinners. Condemning people was part of their daily routine. They had made careers out of ridiculing broken souls. It was the ultimate job security.

The Pharisees were zealous for the law, but they didn't understand the love of God. They imposed judgment without mercy, punishment without love, criticism without understanding.

In the name of hating sin, the Pharisees ended up hating sinners.

Perhaps worst of all, they concluded that their aloofness from sinners was what made them holy. The measuring stick of their goodness was the badness of the people they rejected.

That's why it was difficult for Jewish religious leaders to understand Jesus. They were waiting for a Messiah, a Savior, and they assumed he would be like them. He would wear distinguished robes and be aloof from nasty people. He would walk the streets with his head held high and expect everyone to get out of the way in reverence. They assumed God would come and be just like them.

They were wrong.

Jesus made a point of seeking out sinners and befriending them. He wasn't concerned with his reputation. He wasn't trying to prop up his image by putting others down. He was God and he was perfect, yet he declared by his actions that he did not condemn the worst of sinners.

Ironically, Jesus's harshest words were directed at the sanctimonious Pharisees. He saw through their pseudo-spirituality. He called them out publicly, and they hated him for it. Ultimately, it was the religious leaders who demanded his crucifixion, and they stirred up the crowds until the Roman rulers were forced to carry out their wishes.

Notorious sinners didn't kill Jesus. Religious people did.

The Pharisee in My Head

Before we get too furious at the Pharisees, though, realize that inside each of us is a Pharisee trying to get out. It's happened to me. No sooner do I conquer a bad habit than I become the biggest critic of anyone who still does what I just stopped doing.

I find that righteous indignation comes a lot easier than humility and compassion. Mentally chastising the bad deeds of other people is more comfortable than dealing with my own.

We readily recognize that *other* people have problems. But think for a moment: those evil people most likely don't see themselves as evil. If they start to feel pangs of guilt, they just look a little further down the holiness food chain, find someone worse off, and continue to justify themselves.

So now I have to ask myself, how come I assume I'm near the top of that food chain? And on a related note, who is looking at me and using my mistakes to prop up their self-esteem? Just the thought puts me on the defensive, but it's a fair question.

Here's what I do. I make up laws or rules to fit my standard of living, then I judge you by them. If you follow my rules, you are a good person. If you break my rules, you are a bad person. If you have stricter rules than me, you're a prude who needs to lighten up.

It's so convenient. And so deluded.

If our definition of *sin* is "doing bad things," then we all agree that sin exists. People do bad things. Even if my definition of *bad* differs a bit from someone else's, we still agree that rape is wrong. Genocide is evil. Racial discrimination is appalling.

The problem is that we don't like to include ourselves in

the same category as rapists and murderers. They sin. We just mess up.

When confronted with our badness, we do the *National Geographic* thing: fight or flight. We lash out, pointing fingers and calling people names. Or we hide behind philosophical musings of cosmic good and evil, and we wax eloquent about love and tolerance and how that would make all the bad in the world go away. It's a smoke screen, a defense mechanism to deflect attention from the gaping holes in our holiness.

I don't mean to insult anyone. But freedom starts with honesty. We aren't doing ourselves any favors by defining ourselves as good and others as bad. Let's just agree that we all need help, that we are all in this together.

The good news is that Jesus came to reveal a God who defines us not by our actions but by his love.

Why, then, do I so easily revert to law and rules and regulations when I look at people who are considered disreputable sinners? The ones whose sordid antics are the fodder of TV talk shows, or those who sell themselves for sex on the streets of Seattle every night, or who steal and kill and rape?

I can think of one reason, though I'd rather not admit it: my rules distance me from bad people.

If I separate myself from sinners, I don't have to deal with their pain. I don't have to walk in their shoes or love them or let my heart break with theirs. I don't have to get my hands dirty helping them put the pieces of their lives back together. I can justify rudeness and indifference when my heart should bleed with compassion. I can ignore the fact that but for the grace of God I would be doing exactly what they are doing.

Take it a step further. If I separate myself from sinners, I can afford the luxury of celebrating their punishment. When they get what's coming to them, I feel a sadistic sense of pleasure. They deserved it, after all.

Don't get me wrong. I'm not arguing that we abolish judgment in society—just that we abolish judgmentalism.

If I separate myself from sinners, I don't risk my own reputation. I remain a member in good standing of the holier-than-thou club, where we sit around congratulating each other on how much better we look than everyone else while agreeing that the world is going to hell in a handbasket (whatever a handbasket is) and complaining that the government isn't doing its job very well, and we could do it better if someone would just ask.

Most telling of all, if I separate myself from bad people, I feel better about myself. Because compared to them, I'm doing pretty well.

Again, please don't misunderstand. I don't think rules are horrible. It's how we use them that can be horrible. I have rules for my kids that are for their protection. Our society has laws for our own good. I am completely in favor of authority, order, justice, and structure.

We just have to remember that rules are not proof of our spirituality. If anything, they are proof of our sinfulness, a reminder that we have a tendency toward wrongdoing and that we need help.

The Pharisees were so obsessed with fulfilling the minutiae of the law that they missed the point of the law: to love God and to love others. They thought their sacrifices made God happy while everyone else's sinfulness made him mad. Jesus showed them they couldn't be further from the truth. The sin of the people aroused God's compassion, not his anger. And the sacrifices of the self-righteous meant little to God because their hearts were actually far from him.

Jesus was obsessed with showing mercy to those who least deserved it. He was passionate about giving hope to hopeless people. He was committed to showing grace to the worst of sinners. And if I'm honest, that includes me.

Deep inside, I am painfully aware that I still wrestle with wrong thoughts. I still get impatient with my kids and treat my wife rudely. I still make decisions out of ego and evil rather than love. Whether I am better than you or worse than you really doesn't matter. What matters is that I recognize my need for Jesus.

Rather than rejecting people out of a false sense of superiority, rather than judging and condemning those whose lives don't measure up to my standard of holiness, I need to remember that I am still desperately in need of Jesus's grace.

Jesus befriends the worst of sinners, so Jesus befriends me.

THREE

Friend of Sinners

Jesus went to Zacchaeus's house and became the guest of a notorious sinner. He went to Matthew's house and ate dinner with many tax collectors and other disreputable sinners.

In full view of everyone, he hung out with today's equivalent to pimps, prostitutes, and crackheads. In that culture, to eat with someone was to identify with them. Jesus associated himself with people who were shunned by every upstanding Jew. They were the butts of jokes and the targets of smirks. No self-respecting person would risk befriending them for fear of being found guilty by association.

By everyone's standards, Jesus was a good man. So making friends with bad people didn't make sense. Preaching at them, rebuking them, criticizing them, mocking them—that was expected. Even applauded. But sitting around a table telling jokes and enjoying life together? That was shocking. That was tabloid material.

But Jesus didn't care about the scandal. He cared about the scandalous.

He liked spending time with sinners. He was God and he was perfect, but he spent much of the three-and-a-half years of his ministry hanging out with bad people. He talked with them, ate with them, cried with them, and served them. People weren't just a charity project to him. He cared about them and listened to them. He offered unconditional hope and compassion.

"Healthy people don't need a doctor," Jesus said. "Sick people do." That's why he spent his time with the needy, the helpless, and the depraved. He came down to their level because they could never rise to his. He wasn't out to prove how good he was or how bad they were. He just wanted to offer them hope.

Jesus isn't just a friend of sinners: he is *only* the friend of sinners. Jesus is the friend of people who are willing to admit that they have problems. If we understand that we have issues, if we recognize that we have stuff we cannot conquer, then Jesus is near to us.

You don't have to be good to be Jesus's friend. You just have to be honest.

Where Are Your Accusers?

For many of us, our default view of God is that he is an angry, vengeful deity who is just looking for an excuse to punish us. We would do better to picture him like Jesus—because that is exactly who he is. Jesus said he came to show us the Father. In other words, he modeled God for us. His words, actions, perspectives, and priorities were identical to God's. If Jesus loves evil people, it means God loves evil people. If Jesus is the friend of sinners, it means God is the friend of sinners.

We have to understand something about God: he isn't intimidated by sin the way we are. Usually when someone tells us about something they did wrong, we're like, "You did what? With who? Oh goodness. And then what? How? Lord, have mercy!"

There is a story in John 8 where a pack of religious vigilantes dragged a woman, likely a prostitute, before Jesus. They gloated to him and the crowd around him that she had been caught in the act of sexual sin. Then they asked Jesus what should be done with her. They expected him to pronounce judgment on her. After all, religious law demanded that she be stoned to death for such a sin.

But Jesus didn't throw any stones. He didn't gasp in holy horror. He didn't blush or bluster. Instead, he looked past her sin and saw *her*, and his heart was moved with compassion. Then he turned to her accusers. "Let the one who has never sinned throw the first stone."

Well, when you put it that way . . .

The woman's accusers, ashamed, slipped away one by one, beginning with the oldest. Funny how age has a way of mellowing arrogance.

Jesus looked back at the woman. "Where are your accusers? Didn't even one of them condemn you?"

"No, Lord," she replied.

And Jesus said, "Neither do I. Go and sin no more."

I've been in church a long time, so I'm sure I've read that story dozens of times. But lately, it's actually starting to sink in. Maybe it's because, like that woman's accusers, I'm a little older now, and I'm aware that I'm not such a good person after all. I can imagine myself in her place: trapped by a sordid past,

23

terribly alone, defenseless before a crowd of jeering judges who hold my life in their hands. And then, when hope is lost, the one who truly has the right to condemn me looks at me. In his eyes I read something completely unexpected.

Compassion.

Empathy.

Hope.

We are often harsher judges than God himself. The evil in others arouses our righteous anger, so we don our robes and pound our gavels without ever taking time to hear their stories. We condemn people to life sentences without parole, while God in heaven is saying, "Wait! I love that man. There is hope for that woman. They can be saved."

Can a rapist be saved? A pedophile? A human trafficker? A serial killer? A drug lord? And even if they could be saved, should they be? Seems to us that justice needs to be served.

If justice must be served, we are all in trouble because we all have sin. Maybe we haven't ordered the deaths of thousands because they are a different ethnicity, maybe we haven't raped anyone, maybe we haven't killed anyone—but we are all sinners. On some level, we've rebelled against God.

The fact that Jesus is a friend of sinners is good news for me. Maybe my sins aren't as obvious, but they are just as real. And had I been born in different circumstances, I cringe to think who I would be, what I would have done, whom I would have hurt.

The enemy is not bad people—it's badness itself. And since we all have a measure of badness, who are we to cast the first stone? When it comes to sin, the only one who has a right to condemn others is Jesus. And he refused.

Besides writing off bad people, we too quickly write off ourselves. We swing from the self-righteous side of the pendulum *(That filthy sinner deserves to go to hell!)* to the self-condemning side *(I'm a filthy sinner who deserves to go to hell!)*. Both extremes come from focusing on rules rather than on a relationship with Jesus.

On this journey to understand Jesus, here are the stages as I have experienced them. Each one represents an *Aha!* moment (or an *Oh, shoot!* moment), where I realized I was living on false assumptions of good and evil.

Stage 1. I am a good person, and I am justified in criticizing bad people.

Stage 2. I am a good person, but I should show compassion to bad people.

Stage 3. I am a sinner who needs just as much help as the next guy.

Stage 4. I am loved by Jesus, just as I am, and so is everyone else.

I have to keep reminding myself to live in stage four, because I tend to regress without even noticing.

If Jesus could say just one thing to you right now, what would it be? In my experience, most people would expect correction or rebuke. We think that if Jesus had only one shot at fixing us, he'd make it count by pointing out where we were blowing it the worst.

"You've got to stop losing your temper with your kids."

"Come on, try harder. Work harder. Buck up and be strong. Stop whining."

"You looked at porn again? What were you thinking? Get your life together—or else!"

I think if Jesus had one shot at fixing us, he'd tell us how much he loves us. That's what Zacchaeus experienced. And Matthew. And the woman caught in adultery. And countless other disreputable sinners.

Jesus loves us right now, just as we are. He isn't standing aloof, yelling at us to climb out of our pits and clean ourselves up so we can be worthy of him. He is wading waist-deep into the muck of life, weeping with the broken, rescuing the lost, and healing the sick.

Don't get me wrong—of course sin is bad. Sin hurts us and it hurts others. But the Bible is clear: we are going to sin. Sooner or later, willpower and education and good manners just won't be enough. We'll screw up. So if our hope is in sheer moral fortitude, we are—to put it scientifically—toast.

Jesus sees our sin more clearly than anyone, yet he loves us more than anyone. He's not going to write us off because we had an abortion or are addicted to prescription meds or look at naked people online. Yes, he's grieved by the sin. It's destroying us, and he hates that. But our badness does not change for an instant the overpowering love of God for us. If anything, it makes him that much more determined to rescue us. He will never give up on us, no matter how much we run from him.

No sinner is irreparable or irredeemable. No sin is so great that the blood of Jesus cannot cover it. His love is so deep and wide that he can, in one moment of our faith, forgive our past, present, and future sins. Sin is simply not a problem for God.

As a pastor, I don't want people in my church to hide heroin habits behind a Hugo Boss suit or paint on smiles like makeup so their misery doesn't show. If sinners aren't welcome at my church, then I better find a new church—because I'm a sinner too. And I'm the worst of all, since I know better.

Church is a place where a bunch of people who realize they need help get together to love Jesus and encourage each other. And then something happens: we start to change. God transforms us one area at a time. We hardly know how it happens, but one day we look around and realize that our marriage is working. We like our kids, and they actually like us back. We talk nicer to people and we get mad less often. And we can't take the credit for the transformation, because we just fell in love with Jesus. God did the hard part.

Jesus told the woman accused of sexual sin to "go and sin no more." That wasn't a threat. It was a declaration of freedom. He wasn't interested in condemning her past. He wanted to rescue her future. Jesus knew she didn't want to sin. Who starts out with the goal of being a prostitute or a porn star or a pervert? But difficult situations and wrong choices conspire to trap us in hopelessness. Jesus came to break the cycle of sin and condemnation and to give us back our future.

The Smith Family Mantra

A pastor friend of mine once asked me, "Judah, do you know any pimps?"

"Um, no?" I was a bit confused about where this conversation was going.

"Do you know any drug dealers?"

"No."

"Any crackheads?"

"I don't think so."

"Any exotic dancers?"

"No!"

"How about any prostitutes?"

"Of course not!" I was a bit indignant now, as if he was try-ing to indict me somehow. He got a sad look on his face.

"Neither do I," he said. "I think that's part of the problem."

I might have known some pimps, pushers, or prostitutes, but I wouldn't have known it because I had never taken the time to find out. I had plenty of good friends who were good people, who shared my values and beliefs, who were going in the same moral direction I was. And as a pastor, much of my workweek is spent prepping for church services, preaching to church people, and sitting in church board meetings.

By Jesus's definition, everyone I cared about fit in the "well" category. And I was comfortable with that. I was will-ing to be friendly to the sick—but not to be a friend to them.

Since that conversation, I've determined to open my heart to people whose lives are morally different from mine. Not so I can pity them, rebuke them, make projects out of them, or turn them into a trophy of my evangelism—just so I can be their friend.

Jesus came to seek and to save those who are lost. That's what he told Zacchaeus. His passion was looking for lost, lonely souls and bringing them home to God. He didn't look at lost people as interruptions. He didn't wait for them to wander through the doors of his church and into his pastoral study. He went out into society and found them. He invited himself over to their houses to eat, and he wasn't in a hurry to leave.

His desire to be with sinners amazes me—but even more

amazing, sinners desired to be with him. Typically, really bad people don't like to hang out with really good people, and vice versa. That's why the sinners avoided the Pharisees, and the Pharisees snubbed the sinners. The Pharisees insisted that people meet a strict code of conduct before they could belong to the "in" crowd, before they could be accepted as true Jews. They preached down at people from a pulpit of lofty ideals, imposing standards of behavior they themselves couldn't follow. They alienated the people who most needed their help.

Jesus was different. He didn't wink at sin, but he didn't write sinners off either. He offered faith, hope, and love. That's why time after time in the Bible we find hardcore sinners seated around a table with Jesus, just chilling. They would spend hours listening, asking questions, laughing, crying. They were captivated by his compassion and riveted by his practical explanations of how to do life. Jesus let them *belong* long before they *believed* or *behaved*. He offered them freedom from the issues, hang-ups, and complexes that plagued their lives.

I have a long way to go to relate to people as naturally and effectively as Jesus, but it's one of my goals. I am learning to listen more, to ask better questions, to laugh more readily, and to offer less advice.

My son Zion is in first grade. Every day when I drop him off at school, I say the same thing: "Zion, remember, we are Smiths. What does that mean?"

Then together we repeat this mantra, "We are kind and encouraging, and we look for lonely people."

He rolls his eyes sometimes, as if to say, *Dad, just hurry, I'm going to be late.* He gets that from his mom; punctuality doesn't rate high on my value scale. But people do. They are at the very top, and I want to instill that in my kids throughout their lives.

I realize it's not my job to convince people they are wrong and I am right. It's not my job to change them. That's a pretty arrogant approach to take anyway. When I see myself as a friend rather than a judge or schoolmaster, the relationship is a lot more natural.

Sometimes we are outright rude when we interact with people. We meet a gay guy or a couple living together, and we think we have the obligation and right to warn them what God thinks about their sexuality on our first meeting. As if their sex life is the first thing on God's agenda.

It's not.

Love is. Grace is. Mercy is. *Jesus is.*

I'll be honest—I would be ticked if someone I hardly knew presumed to meddle with my personal life. And I'm a pastor, so I'm supposed to be understanding and gracious and humble. I'd tell that person to mind his own business, that I'm fine how I am, thank you very much. Then I'd write him off as a wacko and avoid him like a prostate exam.

Again, I'm not saying sin doesn't matter, especially if we are dealing with someone who might be harming others. But when sin becomes more important than the sinner, an alarm needs to go off in our heads.

There are no shortcuts to authentic friendship. Relationships are messy and unpredictable. We can't fake love just to get someone to come to church. That's manipulation and hypocrisy, and sooner or later it will backfire.

God shows us what authentic love is in John 3:16, probably the most famous verse in the Bible. "For God so loved the world that He gave His only begotten Son, that whoever believes in Him should not perish but have everlasting life" (NKJV).

God so loved the world. He loved the whole world; not just the good part of the world, the part that loved him already, or the part that he knew would love him back. We need to expand our hearts, our comfort zones, and our friend zones.

He gave his only Son. He was willing to make real sacrifices to build real relationships. Sometimes we need to put aside projects and schedules for the sake of people. Like Jesus, we need to be interruptible.

Whoever. He showed unconditional love and acceptance. Love is risky. We might be rejected. We might be crucified by the people we are trying to help. But ultimately, love will prevail.

Sinful in Seattle

My desire for myself and for my church is that we would see the sinners of Seattle as God sees them. Or better said, as God sees *us*. That we wouldn't point fingers at people or condemn them or try to fix them or try to save them (as if we could), but that we would just love them.

Society already condemns them. Their own thoughts and guilt and shame torment them. What they really need are friends who can show them who Jesus is.

Jesus understood what lost people need; and everywhere he went, crowds sought him out. I'm convinced that if we will be like Jesus in Seattle, Seattle will fall in love with Jesus. When people see Jesus for who he really is, he is almost irresistible.

People are closer to God than we realize, and he is closer

to them. It gets back to the whole rating thing. We assume certain people are far from God when actually they might be closer to salvation than the people we think are near to God. At least the serial sinner realizes, *I'm jacked up! I need help.*

Growing up in church, I somehow developed this attitude that people are really obstinate to Jesus the Savior and that they want nothing to do with him. After all, I imagined, most people think sin is fun and God is boring.

In reality, the majority of people in our city would like to know the Jesus we know. All they've seen is a Jesus who glares down from the ceiling of cathedrals or hangs bloodied on a cross. They've heard he was a good man, a good religious teacher, but do they know he is a friend of sinners? Do they know he's not mad at them? That he lived on earth and understands what they are going through? Do they know he is here to help?

When was the last time we asked someone, "Hey, can I pray for you?" More often than not, even the people in my city—one of the most unchurched regions in America—will accept prayer gratefully.

Most of them have figured out long ago that sin is over-rated. They wish they could do better, that they could be less selfish, that they could overcome sexual temptation, that they could control their tempers.

Does that struggle sound familiar? It should. Can you relate? I bet you can. Because whether we are "good" people or "bad" people, whether we have known Jesus for decades or are just thinking about him for the first time, whether we are pastors or prostitutes—we all need Jesus. We are all seated at a table, surrounded by other sinners, listening to Jesus.

Jesus is the friend of sinners, so Jesus is our friend.

JESUS IS grace.

FOUR

Embrace Grace

I'm a hugger. I like to hug. Growing up, I was taught "hugs, not drugs." But I've noticed that some people are not good huggers. It's not their fault—they obviously never learned how to hug back. You try to give them a warm bear hug, and they turn sideways and bounce you off their hip. Or they hug on the same side you do and you almost kiss. Or they get all tense and rigid, and you feel like you are hugging a mannequin with a robotic arm. Those are awkward hugs.

I remember when I was at a resort with my wife, Chelsea, and we were trying to get into the place where we were staying but we didn't have keys. It was in the middle of the night, probably twelve thirty or so. So this older gentleman came out and opened the door for us. Nice man—he had been asleep, I'm sure, and he came out in his pajamas and let us in. Chelsea wanted to thank him, so she went to give him a hug, and all of the sudden he twitched and jerked like he was having some sort of fit.

Typical guy. No idea what to do with a hug.

That's how we often react when grace comes at us. It's awkward. God offers us something that's too good to be true—unearned, unmerited, total forgiveness—and we stand there, stiff and uncomfortable, waiting for the embrace to stop so we can get back to the business of earning our way into heaven.

We need to embrace grace. We need to learn how to hug back.

Seeing Grace

Grace is hard for most people to define, let alone embrace. The word is found throughout the Bible. In fact, it is arguably the most important concept and term in the Bible. Grace is the foundation of Christianity and the essence of salvation. As such, we should probably understand it.

Webster's has eight different definitions for grace, including these four that you have probably heard before:

- A charming or attractive trait or characteristic ("carry yourself with grace")
- Approval, favor ("remain in his good graces")
- A title of address ("Your Grace")
- A short prayer at a meal ("Say grace over dinner")

Webster's top definition, however, comes closest to the biblical meaning of grace: "Unmerited divine assistance given humans for their regeneration or sanctification."

If you're like me, your eyes glazed over a bit when you read that. I'm sure someone smarter than me was blessed just by reading it, but I need an example, a real-life story, for it to make sense to me.

One thing I love about Jesus is that he spoke in simple terms. He didn't pontificate theologically in order to impress people. He told stories. If he were on earth today, everyone would follow him on Twitter and read his blog because he was real. He was authentic. What he said made sense. It went straight to the heart of the matter.

My favorite story Jesus ever told is what we call the "Parable of the Prodigal Son," which is found in Luke 15. *Parable* is a sophisticated word for a fictional story with a moral, like Aesop's fables. *Prodigal* means "wasteful," but the story of the prodigal son has become so well-known that the term can describe anyone who goes AWOL in an area of life and then returns.

A parable is meant to teach something, so in order to understand this one, we have to see the context in which it was given. In this case, religious people are once again criticizing Jesus because he was a friend of sinners. Luke 15 states, "Tax collectors and other notorious sinners often came to listen to Jesus teach. This made the Pharisees and teachers of religious law complain that he was associating with such sinful people—even eating with them! So Jesus told them this story . . ."

Actually, Jesus told three in a row. All three parables answered the complaints of these religious individuals who said, at least in my brain, "Why in the world would you go to Red Robin and have Cajun Clucks and fries with those shady critters?"

The first story is about a lost sheep. Jesus described a shepherd who leaves the rest of the flock in the safety of the fold and goes into the wilderness to find a lost sheep. When he finds it, he throws a party to celebrate. Then Jesus gave the moral of the story: "In the same way, there is more joy in heaven over one lost sinner who repents and returns to God than over ninety-nine others who are righteous and haven't strayed away!"

The second story is about a lost coin. Again, Jesus described a desperate search for something lost and the profuse joy that follows when it is found. He finished with, "In the same way, there is joy in the presence of God's angels when even one sinner repents."

Side note: when "bad" people turn their lives around, all of us who are "good" should echo the celebration that is happening in heaven. That's why I think we should smile in church—we should dance, we should celebrate, we should laugh, and we should get over our serious selves and represent the joy of heaven.

Another side note: I've heard people say that religion is boring, living in purity is a drag, and they'd rather go to hell because at least they'll be able to party with their friends. Sorry, but that's messed up. If anyone knows how to throw an over-the-top, blow-your-mind kind of party, it's the Creator of the universe, the one who invented fun and pleasure. I'm just saying.

The final story, the parable of the prodigal son, is the longest of the three, but it's worth reading even if you have heard it before.

> A man had two sons. The younger son told his father, "I want my share of your estate now before you die." So his father agreed to divide his wealth between his sons.
>
> A few days later this younger son packed all his

belongings and moved to a distant land, and there he wasted all his money in wild living. About the time his money ran out, a great famine swept over the land, and he began to starve. He persuaded a local farmer to hire him, and the man sent him into his fields to feed the pigs. The young man became so hungry that even the pods he was feeding the pigs looked good to him. But no one gave him anything.

When he finally came to his senses, he said to himself, "At home even the hired servants have food enough to spare, and here I am dying of hunger! I will go home to my father and say, 'Father, I have sinned against both heaven and you, and I am no longer worthy of being called your son. Please take me on as a hired servant.'"

So he returned home to his father. And while he was still a long way off, his father saw him coming. Filled with love and compassion, he ran to his son, embraced him, and kissed him. His son said to him, "Father, I have sinned against both heaven and you, and I am no longer worthy of being called your son."

But his father said to the servants, "Quick! Bring the finest robe in the house and put it on him. Get a ring for his finger and sandals for his feet. And kill the calf we have been fattening. We must celebrate with a feast, for this son of mine was dead and has now returned to life. He was lost, but now he is found." So the party began.

Meanwhile, the older son was in the fields working. When he returned home, he heard music and dancing in the house, and he asked one of the servants what was going on. "Your brother is back," he was told, "and your father has killed the fattened calf. We are celebrating because of his safe return."

The older brother was angry and wouldn't go in. His father came out and begged him, but he replied, "All these years I've slaved for you and never once refused to do a single thing you told me to. And in all that time you never gave me even one young goat for a feast with my friends. Yet when this son of yours comes back after squandering your money on prostitutes, you celebrate by killing the fattened calf!"

His father said to him, "Look, dear son, you have always stayed by me, and everything I have is yours. We had to celebrate this happy day. For your brother was dead and has come back to life! He was lost, but now he is found!"

Three stories. Three lost things. Three parties. Jesus really, really wanted these self-righteous people to understand something: God loves bad people and rejoices when they turn to him.

The Pharisees couldn't believe that God would actually celebrate sinners. Chastise them? Yes. Make them pay for their evil? Without a doubt. But throw a party? What? They couldn't wrap their religious, rule-focused minds around that level of grace. They couldn't hug grace back.

I've heard the story of the prodigal son preached dozens of times. For that matter, I've preached it myself more than once. We preachers usually focus on how dumb the son was and how terrible sin is. But this story is more about the father than about the son. The son wasted his money with extravagant, unrestrained living. The father restored his son with extravagant, unrestrained grace.

Look back at the first two stories. What did the sheep do to be found? He didn't do a thing. If anything, he probably ran farther away. Sheep are dumb like that. Or so I've been told—I've never herded sheep, and it's safe to bet I never will. And what about the coin? What did it do? Nothing. He—or *she*? how do you know?—just hung out with dust bunnies in the corner until the woman found him/her.

We don't preach sermons about how repentant the sheep was or about how diligently the coin sought out his owner. But when it comes to the story of the prodigal son, we like to focus on his humility and repentance, as if that somehow earned him forgiveness.

It didn't. By all counts, he had blown not only his reputation and his inheritance but also his right to sonship. He had scorned his father publicly. When he slogged through the pigsty mud, he dragged the family name behind him.

Yes, his repentance was important, because without it he wouldn't have returned to the father. But his self-condemnation and self-deprecation could never make him worthy of being accepted.

Dear Dad

I have an issue with the little speech he prepared, actually. I can imagine him trying to write it. He has just decided to go back and become a servant in his dad's house because his dad was so good that even the servants always had enough to eat.

But a thought stops him. *I can't just go back with nothing. I've got to have something to say to convince him to take me back.* So he sits down, grabs some papyri, dips a feather in ink, and starts to write a speech.

"Dear Dad. You're the greatest! Sure missed you . . ." *No, that's stupid.* He crumples it up, dips the feather in ink again, and starts to write.

"Dearest Father, if I lined up all the fathers in the world and had to pick one, I would pick . . ." *No, that's stupid too.* Throws it out.

"Hey Dad, sure miss playing catch with you in the back . . ." *No, that's not it either. Just get to the point.*

"Dear Dad, I've sinned against heaven, against you, against everyone, and I'm no longer worthy to be your son. Just make me one of your servants." He folds up the speech, finds a moped, and gets some goggles and a map before heading back to his dad's house.

But stop a moment. Here's my problem with that speech. What does he mean, "I'm no longer worthy"? When was he *ever* worthy?

I have an eight-year-old son, a five-year-old son, and a three-year-old daughter. What if one of them came to me one evening and said, "Dad, I think I've finally done it. I've been super good lately, and I think maybe, just maybe, I'm worthy to be your child"?

I think I'd be a bit ticked, actually. I'd be like, "Worthy? Kid, you don't know what you're talking about. Now go eat the dinner that I paid for. Put on the pajamas that I bought for you. Go sleep in the bed that I purchased for you."

They are my kids. I love them. I would die for them. I'd do anything for them. It's never been about how good or bad they are, and it never will be. Being a son or daughter has nothing to do with being worthy. We are sons and daughters of God by birth, not by worth. That's why Jesus says we must be born again. We must be birthed.

No baby is born as a result of his or her own efforts. The doctor doesn't holler down the birth canal with a megaphone, "Come on, kid, try harder! Work harder! It all depends on you!" The mom works hard, and the dad claims he works hard, but the baby is just along for the ride.

Spiritual birth happens by grace when we believe. Ephesians 2:8–9 says, "For by grace you have been saved through faith, and that not of yourselves; it is the gift of God, not of works, lest anyone should boast" (NKJV).

Believe what? Simply that Jesus exists, that he paid for our sins when he died, and that he rose again to make new life available for each of us. Our sonship is not based on our performance but on Jesus's finished performance and our faith in that finished work.

Some of us knew that we were saved by grace a long time ago, but somehow, somewhere, we got off track. We started to think, *Now that we are Christians, now that we know better, we have to do something to maintain our standing with God.* We have to strive and stress and strain to stay on the straight and narrow.

What? Where did we get that? Jesus died for us before we were born, before we had done anything, good or bad. Why is he going to start making us live by rules and law now?

When Grace Runs

Back to our story. The boy is not even home yet when his father spots him in the distance. The man must have been out on his porch every night for months, maybe even years, making a fool of himself in front of the neighbors, scanning the horizon, hoping against hope to see a familiar silhouette coming down the lane.

"Give it up, man," his neighbors and friends must have said. "Your son hates you. He's lost to you. He's a failure. Stop wasting your time waiting for him. That boy doesn't deserve your love."

But the father never gave up. To him, it had nothing to do with what was deserved, what was fair, or what was expected. It wasn't about a policy or a law. It was about his son. This was personal.

The Bible says, "While he was still a long way off, his father saw him coming." Notice the phrase, "a long way off." We can take all our education, our information, our resources, and our giftings, and we can plan out how we are going to find God and convince him to take us in; but even with all our planning and plotting and preparation, the best we'll ever get is still a "long way off." We'll never make it back to God on our own.

And so the son is coming. He's trying his darnedest. He's on his little moped. *I'm going to find Dad.* He's looking at the map, thinking, *I haven't been this far away from home before. How do I get back to Dad's house again?* He's trying in his own strength.

And then all of a sudden, he sees this man in a long robe and Tevas running at him.

It's Dad.

We think, *Wow, that's nice, the father ran.* I've heard that in the Middle Eastern culture of the day, men didn't run. It was undignified for a man to run, especially for someone of this social standing.

Remember, while Jesus is telling this story, there is a crowd of common folk gathered around him. They are wondering why Jesus goes to Starbucks and has a double vanilla extra hot latte with Mr. Casino Owner. So Jesus explains that this boy was trying to find his dad, and he was still a great way off. And the father *ran* to him.

When Jesus said, "ran," I guarantee that everyone sucked air, because they were thinking, *I never saw my daddy run. Dads don't run.*

What was Jesus trying to communicate?

Crazy love. Super, extravagant, lavish love. Love that overcame the father so much that he lost all good sense and set aside his dignity.

I remember being at soccer practice with my son Zion when he was four. I was on the sideline with Eliott, who was two. Zion started his little scrimmage, which was the most pathetic soccer scrimmage you can imagine. Six or seven four-year-olds, just running around aimlessly. But all of a sudden the ball jumped out of the pack and bounced toward the goal. Zion broke away from the team in hot pursuit. I jumped to my feet, screaming. "Go, Son! Go!" And I started running down the sideline. "Kick the ball in the goal!"

I should mention that there were no other parents at soccer practice. This was basically a substitute for daycare. I'm sure the coach was thinking, *Dear Lord, who is this man?*

Zion was a four-year-old, but you would have thought it was the World Cup of preschoolers, and I was knocking over imaginary cameramen and Gatorade tables as I ran next to my kid. "Kick the goal, Son!" The whole time I was making exaggerated sweeping motions with my foot, just in case he didn't know what I meant.

At this point Zion was looking at me—he's not even looking at the ball—and he was smiling, basking in my pride. Then he accidentally swiped his foot, and the ball bounced off his ankle and dribbled into the goal.

"Yeeeeeaaaahh! Yes! Yes! Wow! That's my boy. Yes!" I screamed shamelessly. I pulled off my shirt and waved it around my head. Then I picked Zion up and paraded him around the soccer arena on my shoulders.

Afterward, sanity returned and it dawned on me what I had just done. The nice college kid who was getting paid by the hour to help my four-year-old bounce the ball off his ankle was looking at me, and he was thinking, *You need attention. You need help. You need Dr. Phil.*

Growing up, I had watched other dads overreact at games. I always swore I wouldn't do that, and here I was at practice—not even a real game, for crying out loud—and I lost my mind. But when they are your own offspring, and they look and act like you, and they put on adorable little cleats and shin guards when they don't even need them, and they get a breakaway in soccer practice—you forget decorum and protocol. I can't explain it. I didn't plan it. I didn't think, *Today I will cheer for my son.* I just got caught up in the moment.

It's crazy love. It's a father's love.

In this parable of the prodigal son, the father represents our heavenly Father—God. He celebrates every little thing we do. He's constantly posting photos of me on a celestial version of Instagram, and the angels are like, "God, what's the big deal? The guy is an idiot."

And God says, "Yeah, he's a funny kid. But he'll grow out of that, and it doesn't matter because I'm so proud of him."

Even in our darkest moments of sin and self-centeredness, God still loves us. No matter what. And the moment he sees an inkling of repentance, he goes crazy. He smothers us in his embrace. He calls for the robe, the ring, the sandals. He throws a party in our honor.

That is grace.

Too Good to Be True

I'm getting ahead of the story. The prodigal son deserved to be punished. Disowned. Banished from his father's presence forever. He knew it, and so did the crowd of people listening to Jesus. But now, before he can walk to his father, his father runs to him. Luke wrote, "Filled with love and compassion, he ran to his son, embraced him, and kissed him." One translation of the Bible says his father "fell on his neck" (KJV). It's a bear hug. He smothers him. He ignores social constraints and constructs, and he covers him with kisses.

The boy is weary, lonely, filthy, broken by life. He stinks. He barely made it home. Now everything within him wants to melt into his father's arms, to be a little boy again with no cares or fears.

But buried in his father's arms, he remembers something. He doesn't deserve this. This isn't right. This isn't fair. That's what logic says, anyway. He tries to wiggle his way out of the embrace so he can give his speech.

You have to understand that the people listening to Jesus's story have been under the tyranny of legalism and law their whole lives. They think exactly the way the boy is thinking. Right about now, though, they are wondering, *Who is this Jesus? How can he speak of such love? The Pharisees and the priests say that you get what you deserve. That you've got to do everything right. That you've got to pray and read the Bible. You have to know all the jargon and be perfect. But this man is speaking of a kind of love I've never heard of before.*

When Jesus talks about the boy's speech, I guarantee everyone listening is thinking to themselves, *Now that's a good speech. That speech is going to work. You watch, he's going to win his dad over with that one.* They're thinking, *Oh, I'll take notes on that speech. I like that.* They didn't get it.

The son squirms free and launches into his plea: "Uh, Dad, I've sinned against you, and I'm no longer worthy . . ."

Midspeech, his dad stops him. He ignores his logic. It's flawed anyway. He calls for servants to bring new clothes and a ring to put on the boy. He decrees a massive celebration in honor of his son.

Honor? What did the son do to deserve honor? That was the question the boy's older brother asked. It was the question the Pharisees and the rest of the crowd were asking. And more likely than not, it's the question you and I ask every time grace runs at us.

He didn't *do* anything. It wasn't about him. It was about the grace of the father. The wayward son simply had to accept the forgiveness the father offered him.

Bewildered but suddenly hopeful, the son enters his father's house. The party starts. People are overjoyed to see him. They welcome him home. There is no shame, no guilt, no rejection.

He looks down at his robe. He twirls the ring on his finger. He slaps his sandals against the floor, just like old times. *Could it be? Could his folly be forgotten just because the father said so? Could there really be a future for him, even after all he had done?* It seemed too good to be true.

That's grace.

FIVE

Grace Is a Person

When someone gives you a gift and says, "Go on, open it! I want to watch!" you should be nervous. In my experience, that's usually an indicator that something bizarre is about to go down. I'm sure you've been there. The person is certain you will love the gift. He or she can't wait to watch your reaction, which may include but not be limited to tears, shouts of joy, and dancing in the streets.

So you open it. And you don't even know what it is. "Oh, wow," you say. It's noncommittal and safe, and it buys you some time to regain control of your facial muscles.

"Do you love it?" they ask breathlessly.

"Of course! Yes! Wanted it. Loved it. Had to have it. How did you know?"

And when they leave, you put it on a shelf in your closet, and you only bring it out when they come over, because you have no idea what to do with it.

Grace Abused

That's what a lot of us end up doing with grace. We don't know what grace is or what to do with it, so we leave it on a shelf most of the time. Then we bring it out when we need to get ourselves out of trouble.

This shallow understanding leads some people to abuse grace. They sin on purpose. They plan ahead to sin. They know better—they know the truth—but they turn their backs on it. Then they plead grace like the Fifth Amendment when they get caught. For them, grace is a way to weasel out of owning their actions. It's the ultimate Christian trump card.

I was a youth pastor for eight years, and I ran across my share of shady dudes who wanted to live like the devil but still call themselves Christians. I'd ask them sometimes, "How are you doing? You staying pure?"

"Not so much. I'm a dude, you know. Got hormones and stuff. But it's all good."

"I'm a dude too. It's not easy, but there's hope. You want to stay pure, right?"

"I don't know, you know? I think I'm okay. Better than a lot of people. Sure, sin's bad and all that, but that's what the grace of God is for."

"Grace of God?" Clearly they didn't get it. "Um, yeah . . . God's grace is there for you. It's there to help you change too. Are you seeing improvement?"

"Not really. Getting worse, actually. But hey, grace of God!" And off they would go, unchanged and unconcerned.

People who flaunt their sin in the name of grace don't know what grace is. They don't know what to do with the gift they've been given, so they make it into something it isn't: a get-out-of-jail-free card, a cover-up, a rug to sweep the nasty stuff under. That's not where grace belongs. That's like putting your bicycle in bed next to you. It doesn't fit there.

If we aren't careful, however, we can overreact. Blatant hypocrisy makes us want to qualify grace, to hem it in with restrictions and rules so people don't abuse it. But in the process, we invalidate the very truths that would set people free.

As I write about the unfettered favor of God, the lavish love that covers bad behavior and embraces bad people, I can hear the concerned voices in my mind: *He'd better not get too crazy with this grace thing. He'd better balance out that grace with some truth. He'd better qualify what he's saying. If he just preaches grace, people are going to start sinning.*

News flash: they are already sinning. People don't need grace to sin. They need grace to deal with the sin they already have.

Lately, I have realized something about grace that has changed my life. It's nothing new—people have understood this for years. It's straight out of the Bible. But it has become real to me, and it has helped a lot of things fall into place.

Grace is more than a principle, more than an idea, more than a doctrine or dogma, more than a cover-up for sin.

Grace is a person.

And his name is Jesus.

Oozing Grace

John, who was one of Jesus's disciples and closest friends, wrote this about Jesus: "We have seen his glory, glory as of the only Son from the Father, full of grace and truth . . . For from his fullness we have all received, grace upon grace. For the law was given through Moses; grace and truth came through Jesus Christ" (John 1:14–17 ESV).

There are several points to note in this short passage. First, Jesus was full of grace and truth. That means that grace and truth aren't enemies. They are on the same side. We don't need to balance grace with truth or truth with grace, because they are both personified in Jesus. If we just get more of Jesus, we will have both grace and truth.

Second, this passage says that the grace Jesus brought replaces the grace Moses gave through the law. Jesus is saying rules are good and the law had its place. But ultimately, the law isn't how we get to God. Grace is.

Most important, these verses say that Jesus was "full of grace and truth," and that from his fullness we have received "grace upon grace." In other words, he embodied grace. He oozed grace. He *was* grace. After people met Jesus, they probably said things like, "That man is different. That man has grace all over him." Jesus gave people a picture of grace. They watched him and listened to him, and for the rest of their lives, they didn't have to wonder what grace looked like. They knew.

My favorite definition of grace is from Jack Hayford, a great pastor and author from San Fernando Valley, California: "Grace is God meeting us at our point of need in the Person of Jesus Christ." In other words, we need help, so God gives us grace. *And his name is Jesus.*

I'm not trying to be redundant—just clear. Jesus is the source of grace, the epitome of grace, the manifestation of grace. Jesus is grace, and grace is Jesus.

If you can picture Jesus, you can picture God. One of the most harmful things we do as humans is define God based on our own imaginations. We come up with fallible, subjective definitions, then we project those on him. So, if we had a lousy father or if we are lousy fathers, we imagine God as a lousy father. If we have experienced rejection and abuse and tyranny from authority, then we imagine that God is rejecting and abusing and lording it over us.

Some of us live in constant fear that God is about to write us off and wipe us out, not because there is a shred of evidence to that effect but simply because we imagine him that way. We feel guilty for our bad deeds, and we are finite beings. So we suppose that an infinitely just God must be infinitely upset.

God is up in heaven asking, "Where did you get that idea of me?"

That's why Jesus came. He told his disciples, "Anyone who has seen me has seen the Father" (John 14:9). Jesus came to reveal the Father. He came to show us God. If you want to know what God thinks of you, or what God would say about your sin, or how God would respond if he were face-to-face with you, just look at Jesus, and you'll know.

Cheating on Chelsea

When we realize that grace is a person, not a principle, abusing grace is no longer an option. It's easy to abuse a principle, to manipulate a system, or to excuse away a doctrine. But it's much harder to abuse a person or violate a relationship.

Chelsea and I have been married for twelve years. She is

an amazing, extraordinary woman. Clearly, I married way out of my league. We are best friends, our romance is hot, and we laugh a lot. I'm looking forward to living the rest of my life with her.

I must confess, however, that my efforts in this marriage pale in comparison to hers. Chelsea is a much better spouse than I am. She's the reason our marriage works. She has figured out how I'm wired, and she uses that to bless me. And maybe to get what she wants. But I feel loved and happy, so it's all worth it.

In these past twelve years of ecstasy, I have never had this train of thought: *You know, Judah, Chelsea loves you so much, she takes such good care of you, she's so loyal and faithful—you could cheat on her and be just fine. She'll take you back. She'll still love you.*

I've never had that thought, and I never will. It's ridiculous. It's repulsive.

Why? I'm not faithful to some impersonal ideal called marriage. I'm faithful to a person. And every good thing she does only reinforces my commitment and my faithfulness to her. It doesn't tempt me to abuse her trust.

When some people hear about grace, the first thing they think is: *So, I can go out and do whatever I want, and God has to forgive me?* They haven't met grace—they've met a concept. They've met an idea. They've heard a nice sermon.

When you look in the eyes of grace, when you meet grace, when you embrace grace, when you see the nail prints in grace's hands and the fire in his eyes, when you feel his relentless love for you—it will not motivate you to sin. It will motivate you to righteousness.

When we meet grace, it becomes the fuel of our faith. We pray, we read our Bibles, we worship, and we live the purest lifestyle we can because we love a person. Allegiance to a doctrine can only last so long, but relationship trumps everything. We'll do anything for someone we love.

Beware of Smurfs

The movie *The Smurfs* came out a while ago. If you haven't seen the movie or the eighties cartoon series it was based on, the storyline revolves around a bunch of tiny blue creatures called Smurfs who live in a magical land where they are constantly being chased by, and then outsmarting, a wizard named Gargamel and his cat. Standout memories include their irritating theme song and their use of the word *smurf* as every part of speech known to man.

"I smurf you."

"It's such a smurfy day."

"All the Smurfs are having a smurf of a time smurfily smurfing around the smurfity-smurf meadow."

And so on.

I was a kid in the eighties, and I remember that some of my friends were not allowed to watch the show. Why? Because clearly, Smurfs were of the devil. That was common knowledge in certain Christian circles. People wrote books and preached messages about it. Smurfs were little blue demons, and Gargamel was a wizard, and there were spells and magic and a black cat. Watching such stuff on TV would surely corrupt a child and lead him down a dark path.

Some people reading this book know exactly what I'm talking about. Others are scratching their heads and wondering what planet I grew up on.

Here is the reasoning. Well-meaning Christians and churches wanted to protect their kids from evil influences. So they created rules to identify what was healthy and what was not. I'm not going to say whether the rules I grew up with were right or wrong, because that's not the point. Were there negative influences kids needed to be protected from? Without a doubt. Did some Christians overreact? Of course.

The point isn't whether my childhood was more deprived or more sanctified than someone else's. The point isn't whether watching *Baywatch* meant you had taken the mark of the beast (if you don't know what *Baywatch* or the mark of the beast are, don't worry about it). The point is this: some of us put too much trust in rules.

Rules are not bad, but they can't save anyone. The best a rule or a law can do is set a boundary and threaten punishment for crossing that boundary. People still decide whether to obey the rule or not.

My parents were much stricter than most parents I knew, but I didn't rebel. I didn't turn my back on God. I didn't feel like I had to go off and try out sin just to see if I liked it.

Why? It wasn't because of rules. It wasn't because of threats. It certainly wasn't because I have such a compliant personality—my parents and now my wife can attest to that. It was because of relationship.

I disagreed with their judgment calls sometimes. And I'm sure I was eloquently vocal about it. But I never doubted their love for me. On some level, I realized their rules actually proved their love for me. Whether the decision was right or wrong was less important than the motivation behind it.

I've watched parents make rules out of fear. They try to use rules to guarantee their kids will stay on the straight and narrow. That doesn't work. That's not what rules are for. Rules are meant to lead us to relationship, not to replace relationship.

Let me throw out a word of caution. Focusing too much on rules and too little on grace tells children that what they do is more important than who they are.

Smurf on that for a while.

These principles aren't just for parenting. This is how our relationship with God works. For God, it's more about relationship than about rules. Far more.

Jesus proved that. He loved sinners—he loved us—long before we ever did anything to deserve it. Then he gave his life to pay for our sin so we could have an eternal relationship with God.

Here's the part that must frustrate God a bit. We take this grace-based, love-filled, amazing relationship, and we build a wall of rules around it. We turn relationship into religion. We quantify, codify, and classify grace until it's more about us than about God.

Sure, we do it out of good hearts. We realize our sin sent Jesus to the cross, and we determine never to sin again. Ever, ever, ever. And we make up rules to keep ourselves far from the edge of sin.

Our solution is also our problem. Is "not sinning" really what it's all about? Is that God's top priority? When we get to heaven, is God going to peruse his celestial spreadsheet and say, "It was close, but your sin-to-holiness ratio is better than the national average, so I'll let you in"?

When we see Jesus face-to-face, sin is going to be the furthest thing from our minds. All we will be thinking about is his grace and love and how happy we are to be in his arms.

When we make up rules because we are afraid people will sin, we end up doing an end run around faith. It's not fear that saves us—it's faith. Fear of failure has a sneaky way of becoming a self-fulfilling prophecy. We focus so much on what we don't want to do that we are drawn to it like a moth to a flame. Or like a mosquito to a bug zapper, since we're in the twenty-first century now.

Make rules and follow rules as needed, but don't focus on rules. Focus on faith. Focus on grace. Focus on Jesus.

Sometimes in our zeal to avoid sin, we set aside the grace we need to do so. Despite the fact that we've made a mess of things in the past, we tell God, "Thanks for forgiving me and all that. Now I'll take it from here!" And we run full tilt into a brick wall. Then God puts Humpty Dumpty back together, and we thank him for his forgiveness, and we do it all over again.

I don't hate rules, but I think we need to keep them in their place. And more than that, we need to recognize the preeminence and sufficiency of grace.

Here's the bottom line: everything that rules can do, grace can do better, and more besides.

Why Rules Are Not Enough

To that end, here are some observations about the shortcomings of rules and, by extension, about the need for grace. They are generalizations, of course, not infallible laws of nature, so don't get too defensive on me. Whether you are a free spirit frustrated by your inability to follow rules or a perfectionist who prides yourself on a straight-A lifestyle, this is for you.

1. Rules Are Often Arbitrary.

Some things are gray, not black-and-white. What to do in these situations comes down to a judgment call. I can't be your judge, and you can't be mine. The longer I pastor, the less prone I am to tell people what to do and the quicker I am to just hug them and pray with them.

If you are looking for a brain-dead list of dos and don'ts to lead a happy, holy life, I can't help. I'm not smart enough to tell you what to do in every circumstance. Or maybe I'm not dumb enough—it depends on how you look at it.

But there is a simple, fail-proof answer. It works for every culture, every time period, every family, every personality type.

Jesus.

When you focus on a person instead of a set of rules, things fall into place.

2. Rules Are Powerless.

Rules just tell us what to do or what not to do, but they don't actually help us accomplish it. If we are not able to follow the rules, we end up feeling condemned and hopeless, which demotivates us and makes it even harder to keep the rules.

The word *grace* in the Bible actually has a dual meaning. On one hand, it refers to God's undeserved favor toward us. Beyond that, though, it refers to God's power at work in us to accomplish more than we could on our own. Grace is God-given power to live differently.

3. Rules Are External.

Rules are restrictions imposed on us by others or by ourselves. They are usually meant to stop us from doing what we want or to motivate us to do what we don't want. In other words, the external rule often opposes our internal desires. That creates conflict and makes obedience difficult.

Rules address behavior, but they don't deal with the heart. They don't adjust attitudes. They don't heal the inconsistencies and fractures deep in our souls that could destroy us in the end.

Grace, on the other hand, is internal. It works on a heart level. Where rules attempt to force us to do the opposite of what we want, grace actually changes what we want. It creates internal consistency and integrity. Doing what is right becomes much easier.

Ever meet people who are so holy that they can't enjoy life and they won't let you enjoy it either? That's not holiness. That's self-importance and legalism. It reminds me of Debbie Downer from SNL. You could be talking about anything from football to the lottery, and they manage to inject a pseudo-spiritual comment that points out how spiritual they are because they don't partake in such earthly pleasures.

When we focus on Jesus instead of a code of conduct, when grace changes our desires so we are internally motivated and not just externally restrained, we become a lot more fun to be around. It's much better advertising for holiness than biting people's heads off. I'm just saying.

4. Rules Point Us Toward Ourselves.

Rules and regulations are more about us; grace is more about Jesus. If all we focus on and think about and work for is checking off our holiness to-do list, we will tend toward arrogance and self-sufficiency. Sooner or later, of course, we'll figure out that perfection isn't sustainable, and we'll swing to the opposite extreme: condemnation. That's no fun either.

Grace points us toward Jesus. It keeps us humble, and it also gives us hope that we can live a good life after all. When we mess up, we don't get emotionally derailed. We get up and try again because we know Jesus is on our side. He's not mad at us or even disappointed in us. He's excited that we are trying, and he is there to help us learn and grow.

5. Rules Are Often Based On Fear.

Most rules are successful only if they have teeth, if there is some sort of reward-and-punishment system in place. We obey because we are afraid of missing out on a reward or because we are afraid of being punished. That is fine in many instances, such as an employer-employee or teacher-student relationship—but it's not a healthy father-child relationship, which is what the Bible calls our relationship with God.

Grace motivates us to live right because it first draws us close to Jesus. As we get to know him more, we want to be more like him. It's natural, it's organic, and it's effective.

6. Rules Emphasize The Negative.

Life isn't about gritting our teeth and doing what is right. If we think holiness means spending the rest of our lives missing out on what is fun because we don't want to go to hell, sooner or later most of us are going to give up and go have "fun," and we'll just hope God is in a good mood when he decides our eternal destinies. Hopefully we'll have a fifty-fifty chance.

Grace focuses on the abundant life Jesus freely gives us. What I give up is completely irrelevant because what I gain is so awesome. Until you've experienced it, it's hard to describe what the goodness of God feels like. But it's as far away from a list of dos and don'ts as you could imagine.

When I was a kid, I thought fast-food burgers tasted incredible. That was mostly because my parents only bought steaks when my sister and I weren't around. Cheapskates. Then one day, I tasted some real steak. My life was forever changed, because there's no party like a red meat party. I'm sorry if that offends you. I would make a terrible vegetarian.

Today, if I had to choose between the Golden Arches and Ruth's Chris Steak House, I'd choose Ruth's Chris every time. No question. And the last thing on my mind as I bite into a buttery bite of medium-rare man-food would be the one-pickle excuse for a cheeseburger I had to give up.

Once you savor God's goodness, sin holds no lasting appeal.

Messy Grace

Before I move on to another topic, I should mention that rules are easier to deal with than grace. That's a big part of their attraction. That's why we keep making up rules even when we can't keep the ones we already have.

Rules are tidy. Grace is messy, unpredictable, unquantifiable. I can hold my life up against a set of rules and easily determine if I'm a good person or a bad person. I can do the same with your life, and I can do it from a distance, without having to mess with relationship and compassion and the grittiness of real life.

Not so with grace. Grace risks its reputation to eat with notorious sinners. It sacrifices its schedule to help hurting people. Grace doesn't allow us the luxury of aloofness. It doesn't get so distracted with doing good things that it forgets about people.

If you choose to live by grace and not by rules, you are in for some messy moments. But once you've embraced grace, you'll never let go.

In case you were wondering, I didn't take my kids to watch *The Smurfs*. Not because I was afraid they would turn into devil-worshippers and sacrifice the neighbors' pets, but because we heard from a family member that the movie was too scary for their kids. My oldest probably could have handled it, but not our second son. So I said no, and we watched some-thing else. I didn't make a big deal about it, but I didn't apologize for it either. I suppose someday they might write a book about me and my tyrannical rules, but I'm pretty sure they will still love me, and that's what counts.

SIX

Leaving Worthy World

Many of us spend all our time in what I call Worthy World. It's kind of like Disneyland. Disneyland's motto is "The happiest place on earth." Worthy World's motto is "You only get what you deserve." That's the first thing they tell you when you check in. It's posted on all the walls. It blares out of tinny speakers all day long.

Worthy World is lame. The paint is peeling on all the attractions. The Ferris wheel is twelve feet tall and gets stuck all the time. Your neck hurts after riding the bumper cars because they jerk so badly. The petting zoo features a scrawny goat and a dog that looks as if it might have rabies. The popcorn is a week old and tastes like burnt grease.

Many of us are still riding the pathetic little rides at Worthy World. We wonder why it isn't more fun, but we can't afford anything else. So we laugh empty laughs and tell each other how great this place is.

And every once in a while, over the fence we catch a glimpse of an amazing place called Grace Land. No, not Elvis Presley's estate. That's Graceland. Grace Land is full of the craziest, most awesome rides ever. We see people who are having the time of their lives on these enormous roller coasters. We look over from our little carousel and wonder what they did to get into Grace Land.

Wow, we think. *Tickets to that park must cost a fortune. I could never get in there. I could never earn that.*

Then someone peers through a hole in the Worthy World fence and says, "Dude, why don't you come over to Grace Land? It's awesome! It's amazing!"

"No, I can't do that. I could never pay for that. I don't deserve that. Grace is not for me."

"Don't you know? Grace Land is free!"

"Free? No, that's not possible. That's too good to be true. Thanks anyway. I only take what I deserve."

That sounds like humility, but it's not. It's false humility, which is just pride masquerading as modesty. Pride is one of the greatest enemies of grace.

You thought Disneyland was expensive? At Worthy World, they'll charge everything you can cough up, and it still won't be enough. But the rides at Grace Land won't cost you a thing. Jesus owns the park, and he says that anyone who wants to can come in at no charge.

We don't have to earn anything. We don't have to pay anything. We don't have to deserve anything. That's what grace is all about.

Finished

Have you ever paid for someone's meal, only to have the person insist on repaying you? A bit of resistance is natural, even polite. But if the person you are trying to bless out of the goodness of your heart absolutely refuses to take your gift, you actually feel dishonored and snubbed.

Some people think that when they receive God's grace to cover their sins, they are taking advantage of him. They know they were saved by grace initially, but they feel as though every new sin is another nail in Jesus's hands. When they mess up and have to ask for forgiveness, they do it with the feeling that they are frustrating God or insulting his generosity.

I respect their sincerity and work ethic, but they are dead wrong.

Grace wasn't free for Jesus. It cost him everything. That is precisely why we should receive it freely. The most insulting thing we could do is reject this costly gift and say, "No thanks, God, I got this." Please don't tell me Jesus was beaten and mutilated and tortured so we could try to save ourselves through our paltry good deeds. Don't cheapen Jesus's sacrifice by trying to pay him back.

When we receive and enjoy his grace, we aren't bothering God. Far from it. That's how he likes it. In God's mind, Jesus's death on the cross solved the sin problem, and now we can get back to the abundant life God originally created for us.

I find the more I get to know Jesus and his goodness, the more I want to live in a way that pleases him. It's that simple.

Sometimes we get way too fixated on how powerful sin is and how weak we are. We worry that if we relax for a second, we'll mess up royally and ruin everything. Ironically, our paranoia only serves to make us more conscious of our sinfulness. It's like staring at a donut and hoping it will motivate us to lose weight.

Then someone comes along and tells us about grace. They tell us God loves us no matter what. They say God isn't nearly as worried about our sin as we are, because Jesus already dealt with sin on the cross. And we think, *I already mess up a lot. If I stop stressing over being righteous, who knows what will become of me. It's a slippery slope straight to hell.* So we hold our holiness in a death grip and we strive for perfection as if it all depends on our performance.

It doesn't. That's the point. That's what Jesus was saying to the crowds, and to his disciples, and to notorious sinners, and to the Pharisees. Our righteousness doesn't depend on our present performance but on Jesus's finished performance.

One of the last things Jesus said as he hung on the cross has been ringing in my mind lately. It is a phrase that changed forever how man relates to God, and it has altered the way I view myself, the way I understand God, and the way I react to sin.

Jesus said, "It is finished."

The more I think about this potent little phrase, the more convinced I am that we need a bigger estimation of God and a smaller estimation of sin. Some of us are so overwhelmed by the enormity of our failures that we can't believe Jesus could love us. That's a problem. That's a far bigger problem than the sin itself, because sin isn't a big deal.

Let me explain. Hang with me here, because I am actually going to get almost logical. Scary thought. Some of you left-brain readers are thinking, *Finally! There is a God!* It might not happen again, so enjoy it while it lasts.

Is sin a big deal? It depends on how you look at it.

Sin has three major components: guilt, power, and effect.

First, the *guilt* of sin refers to my status of "guilty" when I sin or violate a law.

For example, if I park illegally, I am guilty of breaking the law. I can be punished. And if I happen to be in downtown Kirkland, where I live, I will surely be caught and prosecuted to the full extent of the law, because we have a parking-meter monitor who rivals the CIA in stealth and effectiveness. The government would have found Osama bin Laden years earlier if it had put her on the case. She has no grace whatsoever. Maybe I'll give her a copy of this book.

The *power* of sin is another matter. This refers to an inner drive to do what is wrong. It is often called temptation. Something internal pulls us toward something we know to be wrong. In the case of parking illegally, the power of sin is seen in my lack of patience to find a proper parking place and in my disregard for authority. Those are internal issues that, if unchecked, will lead me to do far worse things than park in a fire lane at the mall.

Finally, the *effect* of sin refers to the consequences of what I do wrong. If I park illegally, the effect might be that traffic flow is hindered or a fire truck can't get to a hydrant. Our sin always has an effect—on ourselves, on others, or both. Sometimes the effect is delayed, but sooner or later it will show up. In the case of some sins, the effect is horrific: the sexually abused child, the battered wife, the victim of rape or murder.

We often approach sin backward. We try to control or diminish its effects, but we never deal with its internal power and shame.

God loves us, but if he were to ignore sin entirely, he would be unjust. That's not a viable solution to the sin problem, because God is perfect. Most of us would be in favor of God overlooking our own sin, but when we start to think about God overlooking the sin of, say, a Hitler or a Stalin, we start to see how impossible it is for God to just sweep sin under the rug. If God overlooks evil, then God himself is evil. By definition, a good God must be just and fair.

The solution? Jesus.

By the way, if you haven't noticed by now, Jesus is the answer to everything. Church kids learn this early on.

> **SUNDAY SCHOOL TEACHER:** "Kids, we're going to talk about love today. Do you know who loves you even more than your parents?"
>
> **KIDS:** "Jesus!"
>
> **TEACHER:** "Right! And do you know who died for you because he loves you so much?"
>
> **KIDS:** "Jesus!"
>
> **TEACHER:** "Very good! You're so smart! Okay, now I'm thinking of something that loves its babies a lot. See if you can guess. It's black and white . . . and it swims . . . and it eats fish . . . and it lives at the South Pole . . ."
>
> **KIDS:** [Awkward silence]
>
> **FINALLY, JOHNNY PIPES UP, A LITTLE CONFUSED:** "Uhh, I know the answer is supposed to be Jesus, but it sure sounds like a penguin to me."

Okay, whatever. I thought it was funny.

My point is that Jesus is the solution to everything, especially our sin problem.

On one level, sin is a big deal. But it's not as big a deal as it used to be, and it won't be a big deal at all in the future. Let me explain.

Sin is a big deal when you consider that all sin is rebellion against God. It is a big deal when you realize we are often slaves to our sin, doing things we really don't want to do, because something inside us controls us. It is a big deal when you look around the world and see all the pain and suffering sin causes. And it is a big deal when you realize that death exists because sin exists.

But sin's days are numbered. Evil is on its way out. Jesus's death dealt with the guilt of sin and the power of sin. As we walk with him, we will sin less, and so the effects of sin will lessen too.

Before Jesus, all people could do was try their hardest and offer periodic sacrifices to (sort of) make up for their guilt. They would kill sheep and birds and bulls as symbols of how serious sin was and how guilty they were.

That sounds barbaric to us these days, but it was the best they could do. You might be wondering, *What good did it do to kill an animal? How could an animal's death make up for their mistakes?*

Exactly.

That's why they had to offer sacrifices all the time—daily, weekly, monthly, yearly. And even with all that, they still never dealt with the heart of the issue: their own sinful nature.

The sacrifices were meant to remind people they needed a solution for sin. Ultimately, the sacrifices pointed to Jesus.

Hebrews 10 says, "The priest stands and ministers before the altar day after day, offering the same sacrifices again and again, which can never take away sins. But our High Priest offered himself to God as a single sacrifice for sins, good for all time . . . For by that one offering he forever made perfect those who are being made holy."

Jesus was the ultimate sacrifice. His death was sufficient for all sin, for all time. It replaced the ineffective and insufficient animal sacrifices of the past.

Once again, is sin a big deal? Considering all the above, I have to say not anymore. The problem has been solved. The solution has been provided. The answer has been found. His name is Jesus, and his essence is grace.

Simple Jesus

Whether we avail ourselves of God's provision for sin is another matter, of course. And some of the power and the effects of sin will only be fully eradicated when Jesus returns and deals with sin and evil once and for all. But Jesus is enough. Jesus is sufficient.

Jesus brings hope for a needy world, and it's called grace. "Where sin abounded," the Bible says, "grace abounded much more" (Romans 5:20 NKJV). Jesus didn't come to condemn the world; he came to save the world. If he thinks there is hope, if he believes in humanity, we should too.

Jesus's solution to sin was his own death, and that is where our hope for the world must be placed. We don't trust in our efforts to be good, or in education, or in a better military, or in a more effective penal system. It seems most of Seattle can't even navigate a traffic jam without flipping someone off, so thinking we can achieve world peace by trying harder or educating people is a bit naive. Those things are helpful, but they aren't the answer.

Jesus is.

We have to realize that there is more to life than sin. How much of our lives revolves around sin? Everything wrong with this world, from war to famine to sickness, is a consequence of sin. If we didn't have to deal with sin, how much further along would the human race be?

This book is a manifesto of sorts. It is a simple call to return to a simple faith in a simple person. Jesus is the sum and substance of the gospel. He is the core of Christianity. His grace is available to anyone who wants it. No restrictions. No limits. No conditions.

When Jesus died on the cross, he provided a way for us to access God. He solved the sin problem. He paid for the sins of anyone who chooses to accept him.

Smarter people than me have written books on the doctrine of atonement (which says Jesus paid for our sins) and the doctrine of justification (which says we are made righteous because of Jesus's death). I've read a lot of what they have to say, and as I contemplate the depth of God's grace and the implications it has for each of us, I have been overwhelmed by his grace. God isn't just *willing* to forgive sinners—he is *passionate* about it. Even when we were enemies, even before we had done anything to deserve his love, even though he knew we would sin, he still loved us. Nothing can compare to that grace.

I don't pretend to understand the answer to every theological question. Honestly, no one can. You can't calculate and quantify infinite love. You can't fit it into a mathematical formula.

But you can meet Jesus. He is the personification of grace. His death on the cross and his resurrection from the dead three days later are the ultimate demonstrations of that grace.

We would do well to stop focusing on our sins, our failures, our weaknesses, our pasts, and our legalistic attempts to live in holiness and simply relish the finished work of Jesus. That is where grace is found. That is where we receive forgiveness for the past and power to live differently in the present.

Grace is so simple that we have a hard time believing it could be true. But I'm convinced that unless it's too good to be true, it's not grace.

I think guilt and self-condemnation are the source of most complexities in our faith. We get so introspective and self-absorbed that our failures become more real to us than Jesus. It's not healthy. It's depressing. It's morbid. It's selfish.

Condemnation is a great motivator—for about three days. Then it backfires on us. Eventually our good intentions and human efforts aren't enough, and we sin. We don't do what we want to do, or we do what we don't want to do. Then we condemn ourselves even more, hoping that a bigger dose of guilt will jolt us out of our sin rut. And so the vicious cycle continues.

It doesn't help to tell ourselves, *Don't think about the bad stuff. Don't think about drugs. Don't think about strip joints. Don't think about—*

That's not really the point. Yes, we should avoid thinking about sin. But trying not to think about something is the surest way to keep thinking about it.

That's why you don't just tell your toddler, "Don't put mommy's makeup in the potty." If that's all you say, he'll stand there, staring at the toilet, thinking about the glorious splash mommy's mascara will make. So you close the lid, you shut the door, and—key point here—you give him something else to do. Show him something constructive that doesn't involve toilets.

The point isn't to quit thinking about sin. It's to quit thinking about self and to think about Jesus. It's to become God-conscious, not me-conscious.

Do you know what law does? Law makes us self-conscious. When we are self-conscious, we become sin-conscious. We take our eyes off Jesus, and we focus on our failures, our weaknesses, our shortcomings. And we end up sinning even more because that's all we can think about. But grace makes us God-conscious. When we live by grace, we are continually amazed by the love, goodness, and holiness of God. We think about him, and that motivates us to act like him.

Are you struggling with sin? You don't need more willpower. You need more of Jesus.

Loving Jesus, not avoiding sin, is the focal point of our lives.

Yearbook Day

I graduated from Issaquah High School in 1997. At that point it was the largest high school in the state of Washington, with about twenty-two hundred students. Our colors were purple and gold, which are the truest colors, as opposed to crimson and silver. Cougars fans, take note and repent.

One of my favorite days in high school was yearbook day. I don't know how your school worked, but when we got our yearbooks, they gave us a half day to go around and sign everybody's yearbook. I loved yearbook day—whatever it takes to get people to say nice things about me.

I was well liked, but I remember at times being avoided by some people, even by some of my basketball teammates. I didn't really know why. Maybe they thought I was dorky or weird, or maybe they thought I was better looking than them and they were intimidated by me. I hoped it was the latter.

On yearbook day, I exchanged yearbooks with a couple of dozen people, and then I went home and spent two hours reading what people had to say about me. Because it's all about me, right? That's high school for you.

I was shocked as I read what certain people thought about me. I remember thinking: *If I had known they thought this highly of me, I would have been even bolder to share the love of Jesus.*

I still have my yearbook, and recently I read through it again. What can I say—I guess it's still all about me. Anyway, I remember these guys, and I remember how they acted as if I never existed. And I'm still amazed at what was going on in their heads that whole year of silence.

One guy wrote: "Judah, you're truly the most extraordinary young man I've ever met."

What? High school guys don't even talk to each other like that.

He continued, "You're an inspiration to me and all Christians alike. I have the utmost respect for you. Your daily devotion and love for Jesus helps everybody around you."

FYI, this guy never talked to me. Never. I was dead to him. He wasn't serving Jesus in high school until the very end. But he watched me from a distance and looked up to me. If I had only known, I would have been a lot less insecure.

Here's another one: "Judah, you're probably the person I respect most at this school."

I wish you knew this guy. This is unbelievable.

He continues, "You have your beliefs and you stick to them. That's awesome."

Wow. It wasn't awesome when I sat by myself sometimes in the lunchroom. Didn't feel awesome.

"I'm so glad we spent time together."

I'm trying to remember when that was. I tried to, but he was never available to hang out.

"I hope we can hang out or go golfing this summer. Give me a call if you need a fourth for golf. You're one heck of a quarterback too. Sophomore football was fun. I've learned a lot from you, and thanks for everything you've done for me. Friends for life."

I remember sitting at home in my bedroom reading my yearbook, looking at the names and pictures, thinking, *There is no way this person thinks that.* Had I known they respected me, had I known so and so thought I was the most extraordinary young man he had ever met, I would have walked through the halls like a more extraordinary person.

I wonder what God would say if he could write in our yearbooks. I think most of us, when we think of God penning his perspective of us in our yearbooks, expect what I expected from my friends: "Hey, you're an okay guy." "You're kind of weird." "Dude, leave me alone." "Get a life." "Get your act together."

There is a way for us to get God's perspective of us. It's called the Bible—but most of the time we skim the grace parts and highlight the sin parts.

If Jesus wrote in your yearbook, I think you would be blown away by what he really thinks about you. I think you would live differently because Jesus is crazy about you. He is obsessed with you. He is proud of you.

This understanding could literally help your posture. If you think the God of the galaxies and solar system is mad at you, it could be a bit of a burden. It might affect your mood.

"Hey man, what's wrong?"

"Oh, the Creator of everything is furious with me. He might kill me any second."

Well, I'd be down too. That's a weight to carry if I ever heard of one.

Contrary to popular opinion, God is not mad at us. We can hurt God. We can grieve God. But his wrath against sin was appeased by Jesus's death. For those who accept that sacrifice by faith, he no longer looks at our sin. When he sees us, he sees his Son.

When Jesus was baptized, God shouted down for all to hear, "You are my dearly loved Son, and you bring me great joy" (Luke 3:22).

God is just as pleased with us as he is with his Son.

That's not exaggeration. That's not blasphemy. It's the truth. It's Bible. John wrote, "Love has been perfected among us in this: that we may have boldness in the day of judgment; because as He is, so are we in this world" (1 John 4:17 NKJV).

In other words, when God sees us, he sees Jesus. We have the same standing before God as Jesus. We aren't God, of course, so there is a distinction. But when it comes to our righteousness, we are just as pure as Jesus.

Grace is a difficult concept for us humanoids to embrace because we have to live with ourselves. We are painfully aware of our weaknesses and shortcomings. So we are usually hardest on ourselves. It's amazing how many people can accept others but are still trying to find a way to accept themselves.

Sometimes our brains are our own worst enemies because grace isn't logical. It doesn't work on a cause-and-effect basis like everything else in life. From our childhoods, we learn cause and effect. For every effect there is a cause. An apple falls. That's an effect. *There must be a cause*, thought Sir Newton. *Ergo, gravity.*

The other day I was teaching a membership class at my church, and I fell off the platform. I always stand with my feet half off the edge, and people make fun of me for it, but in fifteen-plus years of preaching that way, I had never fallen. This particular class, I was leaning forward to read a verse that was up on a monitor, and gravity took over. It was a graceful fall, as falls go, and the only damage was a sprain in my pride. The clip will not appear on YouTube because my media team loves me too much—and because I give them their paychecks. That's cause and effect too.

When it comes to grace, there's just effect, at least as far as humans are concerned. We didn't do anything to cause it. It's already been caused, and we should just enjoy it.

We put a lot of effort into trying to cause it, however, because that's how we're wired. We are cause people. If there is effect without cause, we feel deep consternation, because that doesn't fit with everything we've known since we were toddlers, when we discovered gravity the hard way.

Because logic gets in the way when we talk about grace, we limit the scope, the magnitude, and the significance of grace. We try hard to comprehend it in our humanness, in our shortsightedness. We get out our logarithms and algorithms and try to reason grace out.

Grace, though, is supernatural by definition, so it transcends our ability to reason and comprehend and calculate. It's bigger than our minds. It's bigger than our understanding. God's ways are higher than our ways. His thoughts are higher than our thoughts. He is God and we are not.

Wide Open Spaces

Remember the woman caught in adultery, the one the Pharisees wanted Jesus to condemn to death? She knew she was dead. She knew there was no hope. Her accusers had her hemmed in, and there was no escape. Her sin defined her and condemned her.

Then Jesus told her accusers that whoever had no sin should throw the first stone. The oldest Pharisee was most aware of his weakness, so he hung his head and slunk away first. Then the next oldest left and the next oldest, until finally even the young, arrogant dudes were forced to admit their own shortcomings, and they, too, sneaked off in embarrassment.

Jesus turned to the woman.

"Where are your accusers? Didn't even one of them condemn you?"

"No, Lord," she replied.

"Neither do I. Go and sin no more."

In one instant, the woman went from total condemnation to total freedom. I'm sure her posture was different when she walked away. Her self-confidence was restored. She had found hope for a better life.

Romans 5 says:

> Therefore, since we have been made right in God's sight by faith, we have peace with God because of what Jesus Christ our Lord has done for us. Because of our faith, Christ has brought us into this place of undeserved privilege where we now stand, and we confidently and joyfully look forward to sharing God's glory.

The Message, a paraphrase of the Bible in modern English, renders that last part this way: "We find ourselves standing where we always hoped we might stand—out in the wide open spaces of God's grace and glory."

"Wide open spaces"—what a picture of grace! Not hemmed in or closed in by sin, but wide open and free. That passage says we have been made right in God's sight. He has set us in a place we didn't deserve, a place of freedom and abundance.

I've heard about grace my whole life, but it's only been in the last few years that I have begun to understand the incredible implications of grace. I've been on a journey of discovery that I am in no hurry to finish. I am passionate, almost desperate to understand what grace means for my family, my church, and my city.

It seems every time I open my Bible these days—even though I'm reading passages I've read many times before—all I can see is God's amazing grace. Every time I pray, all I can think about is how good God is and how Seattle needs to know about his goodness. Every sermon I preach, no matter the topic, always comes back to the grace of God in Jesus.

My mission has become to remind my church that Jesus is still the answer.

Grace is Jesus, and Jesus is enough.

JESUS IS the point.

SEVEN

Come to Me

This isn't a very spiritual thing to admit, but I like to sleep. A lot. Rest and relaxation are high on my priority scale.

This is especially true in the morning. I know pastors who thrive on early-morning prayer meetings. By "early morning," I mean before the Holy Spirit is even awake. They get up, get dressed, get breakfast, and get to church by six o'clock in the morning, and they have the sweetest, most spiritual dispositions as they lead their flocks in prayer.

At six in the morning, I am of no use to God or anyone else. Except for maybe the devil, because I act more like him than anyone else at that ungodly hour. My idea of an early-morning prayer meeting is ten in the morning. I'm feeling that one. That's a word from God.

I've been in more churches than you've been in McDonald's. I always hear preachers say things like, "I was up at five thirty this morning just praying and reading my Bible, and it was awesome."

And I'm thinking, *Man, I'm going to hell.* Because if anyone tried to wake me up that early, I'd cuss at them. I know I would.

If I had my way, the world would not begin in the single digits. The single digits are for my wife and me, for our kids, for breakfast, for time alone with God and family and self. I will see you at ten o'clock or later, and I will be a sanctified, holy man, just as you expect.

I get asked a lot, "Judah, what's your favorite verse in the Bible?"

I always get a bit suspicious, because maybe it's a trick question. Maybe my favorite verse isn't as spiritual as your favorite verse. Inside I'm wondering, *I don't know, what should it be? You go first.*

Here's a question I never get asked. "What's your least favorite verse?" I've actually thought about that. Maybe I'm on thin ice here, because it's the Bible, and we are supposed to like all the verses. But I can tell you exactly what my least favorite scripture in the entire Bible is. It's Proverbs 20:13. "Do not love sleep, lest you come to poverty. Open your eyes, and you will be satisfied with bread" (NKJV).

That's my least favorite verse. If that disappoints you, I'm sorry. But I bet you can relate, so don't get too religious on me. Maybe you need to reread that last chapter on grace.

I also don't like the passage that says Jesus got up a long while before daybreak and went and prayed. Really? What did he have to go and do that for? He was God. Couldn't he just sleep in and encourage us mortals a bit?

So, I like sleep. I don't love it, because the Bible says not to. I just like it. A lot.

Proverbs has another verse on sleep, and this one is more

to my liking. Proverbs 3:24 says, "You can go to bed without fear; you will lie down and sleep soundly." That's the verse I'm holding on to.

Lawmakers and Lawbreakers

Actually, sleep is a good thing. Sometimes we get so super-spiritual and wound up about life, and what we really need is some rest. If some of us got eight hours of sleep for once in our lives, we'd be more like Jesus.

You probably already guessed this, but one of my favorite passages in the Bible has to do with rest. It does more than just encourage rest, however; it redefines how we are to live. It teaches us about a spiritual rest, a freedom from busyness, anxiety, and fear. These verses have revolutionized how I think. They are found in Matthew 11:28–30.

> Then Jesus said, "Come to me, all of you who are weary and carry heavy burdens, and I will give you rest. Take my yoke upon you. Let me teach you, because I am humble and gentle at heart, and you will find rest for your souls. For my yoke is easy to bear, and the burden I give you is light."

When Jesus spoke these words, he was talking to crowds of people who had grown up under the Jewish religious system. This was a system defined by law. People related to God based on law. They related to each other based on law. They carried out business and raised their families and lived their day-to-day lives based on law.

When we think of the term *law* today, we think of government-imposed restrictions. But to Israel, law meant more than not driving your camel too fast in a school zone. It referred to the law of Moses.

Around fifteen hundred years earlier, God, through Moses, gave the Israelites a series of laws that dealt with religious, moral, and practical issues. These laws were designed to help Israel maintain a high moral standard. Israel was surrounded by nations that practiced things like human sacrifice, incest, and ritual prostitution, so the Law was God's provision to help people live better lives.

The most famous of these laws were the Ten Commandments, but that was only the start. The law of Moses was much more detailed than that. It affected every area of life. The Israelites were commanded to keep this law down to the smallest detail, and if they failed in any way, they were guilty of sin. Because no one could keep all the law all the time, they had to offer continual animal sacrifices for sin, as I mentioned earlier.

To make matters worse, in the centuries leading up to Jesus, the Jews had added several hundred additional laws to the law of Moses. This body of laws, which was essentially tradition, was meant to help people fulfill the original law of Moses by controlling their daily lives even more. It was an incredibly detailed set of restrictions and stipulations, and it was the Pharisees' self-appointed duty to interpret and apply this law to everybody's lives.

In the last chapter, we discussed rule-based living as opposed to grace-based living. This is exactly where Israel had ended up. That wasn't God's intent when he gave them the law—it was just human nature.

You Look Tired

I hate it when people tell me, "Judah, you look tired." That's a backhanded way of telling me I look terrible.

"Gee, thanks!" I wish I could say. "You look terrible, too!" But I'm a pastor, and pastors don't tell people in their congregations they look bad.

When Jesus came on the scene, people were stressed-out and worn-out trying to please God. They were so busy trying to do good in order to be good that they couldn't see how good life was. They couldn't enjoy God because they never quite measured up—they always needed a little more holiness and a few more good deeds before God could accept them.

They saw God as a legislator, a judge, a law-enforcer, a cosmic policeman who was obsessed with keeping people in line. That was why, as we discussed earlier, people reacted so strongly to Jesus's apparent indifference to sin. He claimed to be God, yet he didn't slap cuffs on anyone. He didn't hand out parking tickets or death sentences. He just loved people, and he offered them full and free access to God.

When Jesus said, "I will give you rest," people gasped. It was a blast of fresh air in a law-stifled atmosphere.

"Rest? Really? What does he mean? I thought serving God was hard work."

Jesus promised an easy burden and a light yoke, which was a reference to the yokes farmers placed on oxen and the burdens they bore. Jesus was saying that he came to make life easier.

That was the opposite of what the people had experienced. For them, the law was a heavy yoke, an impossible burden. Religion was about trying harder and doing more. It was about pulling yourself up by your bootstraps. Good people were self-made people, people who knew how to suck it up and work harder.

Sounds a lot like our culture today. Christians and non-Christians alike are obsessed with being good people. We buy self-help books and DVDs, we go to seminars, we get counseling, we make New Year's resolutions, we Google our defects and our bad habits hoping to find a cure; we are convinced that if we try hard enough, we can perfect ourselves.

We are worn out and desperately in need of rest. Not physical rest. We need spiritual rest. We need peace with God and with ourselves.

The Rant on the Mount

When Jesus told the people he was the ultimate source of rest, I think something clicked in their minds. You see, this wasn't the first time he had talked to them about burdens and law. But the previous time, he wasn't nearly so encouraging. Backtrack in Matthew to chapter 5.

Matthew 5 is the beginning of Jesus's most famous sermon. It is called the Sermon on the Mount because he preached it from a mountainside so the crowds could hear him better.

This particular part could have been called the Rant on the Mount. Something is clearly bugging Jesus. He says:

> Don't misunderstand why I have come. I did not come to abolish the law of Moses or the writings of the prophets.

No, I came to accomplish their purpose. I tell you the truth, until heaven and earth disappear, not even the smallest detail of God's law will disappear until its purpose is achieved. So if you ignore the least commandment and teach others to do the same, you will be called the least in the Kingdom of Heaven. But anyone who obeys God's laws and teaches them will be called great in the Kingdom of Heaven. But I warn you—unless your righteousness is better than the righteousness of the teachers of religious law and the Pharisees, you will never enter the Kingdom of Heaven!

He had their attention now. Who could possibly be more righteous than the religious teachers and the Pharisees? They were the epitome of religiosity, the pinnacle of perfection. And they let everybody know it too.

The common, everyday guy was shaking his head right about now. "Righteousness that is greater than that of the Pharisees? I'm in trouble."

Jesus is just getting warmed up. I won't quote the rest of the chapter here, but it's strong stuff. Jesus breaks down what it means to be righteous and perfect on a practical, day-to-day level.

His message could have been subtitled, "But I Say." He goes through a list of topics, and for each one, he starts out, "You have heard . . ." and then he quotes a common explanation of the law. Then he follows with, "but I say" and he basically says that what they had been taught—though it was strict—wasn't strict enough. God wanted more.

These were more than pet peeves. Jesus wasn't being

picky. He wasn't having a bad day. He had grown up in this culture, and he knew how people got around God's commandments. He had seen them justify their injustice and sanctify their sin with shallow, religious-sounding arguments.

And he's going to call them out. Right now. In public. From the top of a mountain.

He starts out, "You have heard it said, 'Do not murder.'"

And everyone is thinking, *I'm good on this one. I haven't murdered anyone. Wanted to, maybe, but never did. I'm good. I'm off the hook.*

Jesus continues, "But I say, if you are even mad at someone, you deserve judgment. If you call someone an idiot, you should go to jail. And if you curse someone, you might wind up in hell."

The crowd got silent. Awkwardly silent. You could have heard a pin drop—or a fish-bone sewing needle, or whatever they used back then.

What? they are thinking. *I can't even get mad at my neighbor? Clearly Jesus doesn't know my neighbor.*

Jesus is just getting started. "And you have heard it said, 'Do not commit adultery.'"

Again, people breathe easy. Adultery is one of the big sins, the nasty sins, and they know they haven't committed that one. *I haven't hooked up with any desperate housewives,* the guys are thinking. *I don't even go to Hooters.* They look at their wives and assure them. "No worries, babe. I'd never cheat on you."

"But I say, if you even look at a woman lustfully, it's as if you've already slept with her."

Some guy in the back almost chokes on his flatbread.

He's got a copy of the latest *Fisherman Illustrated* swimsuit edition poking out of his knapsack. Men are looking around saying, "What? I'm a guy. That's what guys do. Doesn't he get it? Now there's not one virgin among us. We're all adulterers."

Jesus continues. He's relentless, brutal, merciless. He touches on divorce, on revenge, on enemies. Each time he points out that even if they thought they were righteous, they were only fooling themselves.

He finishes with, "You have heard it said, 'Love your neighbor but hate your enemy,' but I say, love your enemies and pray for those who persecute you."

"What?" They look at each other. "Pray for those who attack me? I'll pray, all right—'Lord, destroy them all!' That's my prayer. What's he talking about? Love them? That's crazy."

People are not shouting Jesus down during this sermon. They are not yelling "Amen" or waving their handkerchiefs. By this point, they have figured out that the "But I Say" rant is not a feel-good sermon. It is not encouraging. In fact, it is downright depressing.

And in case someone made it through the message without having his or her self-righteousness rocked, Jesus caps it off by saying, "But you are to be perfect, even as your Father in heaven is perfect."

There is a rousing round of silence. People are thinking, *It was hard enough to be righteous before. I could barely keep up with everything the Pharisees told me do to. But this? This is impossible.*

Exactly.

That was the point.

Your Face Looks Funny

Jesus wanted them to know that if they intended to live by the law, they couldn't just pick and choose the parts they liked in order to feel good about themselves. They had to follow all the law or they might as well not follow any of it.

Jesus wasn't being mean. He was showing them their own inconsistencies. In their hurry to be good, they had redefined holiness so they could fulfill the law on their own. They had moved the goalposts. They had found ways to justify themselves in their own eyes. They had deluded themselves into thinking they could be perfect.

The biggest problem with that was not that they were still sinning. God was used to that. It was that they thought they were righteous. They thought they were good enough to get into heaven on their merit. (At least the "good" people thought this—the "sinners," as we saw in the first chapter, had given up long ago.) Self-righteousness is one of the greatest hindrances to relationship with God.

Bottom line: they had missed the point of the law. They thought the point was being good and doing good. But it wasn't.

The point was Jesus.

Deep inside, people knew they weren't righteous anyway. They knew they needed another way. It was never possible to fulfill the law. Jesus wanted them to come to the end of themselves so they could discover the grace that God freely offered through Jesus.

God knew Israel could never keep the whole law. That's why he instituted an elaborate system of sacrifices from the very beginning. The law was not meant to perfect people, just to lead them toward God.

As Jesus preached the Sermon on the Mount, people realized they needed a better righteousness than they had. Their holiness wasn't good enough. Their attempts to be good were pathetic and full of holes. What, then, were they to do?

Remember, this is Matthew 5. If you read straight through to Matthew 11, you would see Jesus's point. He was setting them up to understand a truth that would set them free.

"Come to me," he says in Matthew 11:28. "Are you weary? Are you carrying a heavy burden?" That was everyone listening, you realize. "Come to me, and I will give you rest. My yoke is easy; my burden is light."

This was music to their ears. They were tense and stressed, straining to live holy lives, and it wasn't working.

Ever wonder why some Christians are so grumpy? Often it's because they are so worried about their own sin—or about everybody else's sin—that they can't enjoy life.

"Dude," people ask, "why are you so uptight? Your face looks funny."

"I'm not uptight! What makes you think I'm uptight?" they snap back. "I just really want to sin, but I can't, so my face looks like this because I'm trying so hard not to sin."

"Wow, lighten up. A little sin might do you good." And they make a mental note to never be a Christian.

If that's you, do God a favor, and don't advertise that you are a Christian. There is nothing more uncomfortable for people than a constipated Christian.

For Israel, the law was never meant to be about the law. It was about Jesus. It pointed to Jesus. In John 5:39, Jesus says to the Pharisees, "You search the Scriptures because you think they give you eternal life. But the Scriptures point to me!"

Jesus was the fulfillment of the law. That's why he could say he came to accomplish the purpose of the law. All the law, the prophecies, and the teachings that the Israelites studied day in and day out pointed to Jesus.

God wanted people to do their best, of course, but ultimately he wanted them to know they needed a Savior, a Messiah.

The same principles hold true today. God doesn't want us to just try harder, work harder, and get busier. He appreciates our efforts, but when we make life about doing good and being better, when we make holiness an end in itself, we miss the point.

House of Hypocrites

Being a Christian is not about being good. It's about relationship. About grace. About Jesus. Jesus is the point of life.

That's where true rest comes in. We will never be at rest as long as we are carrying the burden of trying to please God by our good deeds. That is as impossible as it is unnecessary. Jesus was the only one who could, and he already did it, so we need to learn to rest in his completed work.

I've heard Christians talk about the "be perfect" verse we just looked at, and they say, "See? With Jesus, the requirements are even higher than under the law. So you better get busy. You better get your holy on. You have a long way to go, brother."

It's amazing to me that sometimes we leave church more obsessed with self than when we came in. That should never be the result of the gospel. When you've heard the gospel, you get obsessed with Jesus, because it points to him.

"We shouldn't be like the scribes and Pharisees," people say. "We shouldn't be hypocrites. We have to make sure we are more righteous than they were."

Where do we get these ideas? Let's not fool ourselves. We are already hypocrites. All Christians everywhere are hypocrites. I don't mean to insult anyone, but think about it. If we preach one thing and live another, that's hypocrisy, so we have all been hypocrites at one time or another. We might as well rename our church the House of Hypocrites.

When it came to holiness, the Pharisees were professionals. They had memorized the first five books of the Old Testament, which included hundreds of laws. They spent the day planning and plotting how to fulfill every detail of the law. Like the Israelites of the day, most of us don't stand a chance of being as holy as they were, much less being holier. We can work ourselves to the bone attempting to please God, but we will fail.

I'm the biggest hypocrite. Hypocrisy is an occupational hazard for preachers, because we talk so much. I've preached to my church about the importance of loving your spouse and being patient and controlling your words—and then on the way out of the door, I find myself snapping at Chelsea.

I'm not excusing myself, because it is wrong and I'm embarrassed I still struggle with my big mouth. But I'm not going to adopt an attitude of false humility: "I'm not worthy of being a pastor. I will never preach again." I was never worthy in the first place. It's not about me. It's about God, about grace, and about helping people in my church and my city meet Jesus.

Here's another confession: A couple of years ago, I looked

at porn. It was Japanese animated porn, to be specific. I didn't even know such a thing existed. Who comes up with this stuff, anyway?

In my defense, I didn't intend to look. At least not at first. I was stuck in the back of an airplane, flying across the Pacific, when I noticed the guy in front of me was watching anime on a portable DVD player. I like art, and I had heard of anime and was curious what it was all about, so I looked between the seats at his screen. It seemed like a harmless cartoon—until people started taking their clothes off.

Inside, I was thinking, *I shouldn't be watching this. This is probably bad.* But I kept watching. Just to be sure it was really bad. I saw about fifteen seconds' worth before I made myself turn away.

You might be laughing. "Fifteen seconds? What's the big deal?"

Or you might be scandalized. "He's a pastor, and it took him fifteen seconds to decide to look away? I want a refund on this book."

The point is that I looked, even though I knew I shouldn't. I felt terrible about it afterward. Chelsea was sitting in another row the whole flight, and when we landed, I told her the story.

"How long did you watch?" she asked.

"Maybe fifteen seconds."

Dramatic pause. Then, "Alright, you are forgiven. But you better be glad it wasn't twenty seconds, because that would be the end of our marriage." I think she was making fun of me.

That was on a Friday, and that weekend I had to preach several times. I was frustrated with my sinfulness. Part of me wanted to beat myself up over what I had done, to inflict shame and punishment on myself until I had proven how contrite I was. Who was I to preach about God and holiness when I couldn't even control my gaze for fifteen seconds? Maybe I wasn't the right guy for this job.

Actually, self-inflicted punishment in the name of religion feels good, in a sick sort of way. You feel like you are paying for your sin. It's less embarrassing that way. You don't feel so in debt to grace.

But it's futile and unnecessary. Why insist on paying for what Jesus already purchased?

That weekend I made a conscious decision to rest in the grace of Jesus and to believe in his forgiveness. It wasn't "greasy grace." I wasn't denying my sin. I wasn't justifying ongoing sin in the name of grace.

It was the truth. Biblical, theological, doctrinal truth. I was righteous. I was forgiven. My church and my family didn't need me to beat myself up, to refuse to let God use me, just because I didn't feel that I deserved it. They needed me to "be strong in the grace that is in Christ Jesus," as Paul told Timothy (2 Timothy 2:1 NKJV).

I preached a good sermon, if I do say so myself. Ironically, it was on grace. I told the whole church about my fifteen-second fling. Some of them gasped. Some of them got red-faced. Most of them appreciated my transparency. Hopefully none of them went out and rented anime porn.

I wasn't bragging and I wasn't self-condemning. I was honest. Then I talked about the struggle with condemnation that we all face. I don't want to pretend I am holier than anyone.

I want to start resting in the righteousness that is freely and instantly available to us all through faith in Jesus.

Don't get me wrong—I'm not suggesting we care less about holiness. I'm suggesting we care more about Jesus.

Jesus fulfills the law for us. When we put our faith in him, we are made righteous. We can't drum up enough willpower to be perfect, and we don't have to. Jesus already did. I can say that I have fulfilled the law in its entirety. I have carried out all the demands of the law to the fullest. I haven't, of course—but in Jesus I have. I will never be more righteous than I am today.

Infinity Times Infinity

When God looks at me, he says, "That man is righteous." That's just who I am, and I can't change who I am. Even if I haven't prayed in six days, I am righteous. Even if I'm struggling with sin, I am righteous. Even if I don't feel righteous, I am righteous.

Some of us need to go out and get a stamp made that says RIGHTEOUS, and every morning, we need to stamp our forehead with it. Get it made backward so that when we look in the mirror we can read it.

Our good deeds are good, and God is proud of them, and they make the world a better place. So by all means, don't stop doing them. Just don't trust in them for righteousness. That takes the fun out of everything.

Jesus is infinitely righteous, and we are as righteous as he is. So any attempt to make ourselves more righteous by our good deeds would be like trying to one-up infinity.

Remember that childhood reasoning?

Maybe you were arguing with your brother about who was the smartest. "I'm a thousand times smarter than you."

"Well I'm a million times smarter than you."

"I'm infinity times smarter."

"Oh yeah? I'm infinity plus one times smarter."

"Actually, I'm infinity plus a million. Plus one."

"I'm infinity times infinity. Ha! You can't beat that!"

We don't need to play that game. If we have faith in Jesus and his work on the cross, then we are as righteous right now as we ever need to be. We can't add to it, and we can't take away from it.

We are righteous enough to walk into heaven, right up to God's throne, and ask him for whatever we need. That's not what I say—that's what the Bible says. "So let us come boldly to the throne of our gracious God. There we will receive his mercy, and we will find grace to help us when we need it most" (Hebrews 4:16).

Proverbs says that a righteous man may fall seven times, but he rises again. Did you catch that? He's righteous, yet he falls. It's not his perfect track record that made him righteous. The guy fell seven times. He's a klutz. He's a failure.

The man is righteous because God said he's righteous. He's righteous because he trusts God to make him righteous. And because he knows he's righteous, he attempts great things, crazy things, and he never gives up.

We get in such a hurry to perfect ourselves because we think that as soon as we do, God will love us more. But he will never love us more than he does right now. He will never accept us more than he does right now.

God is not in a hurry to fix us. Our behavior is not his

first priority. We are his first priority. Loving us is his main concern.

Our fight against sin is noble and good, but make no mistake: we are not fighting to become righteous. We are already righteous. We are simply learning to live outwardly like the people we are inwardly.

EIGHT

The Meaning of Life

If you are even a little bit introspective, you've probably wondered what the point of life is. *Why am I here? What is life all about? What will make me happy, satisfied, and fulfilled?*

Maybe it was late at night. You couldn't sleep, and you started to ponder the meaning of life. Maybe it was after a loss or a failure, and you were forced to ask yourself what you were doing with your life. Or maybe it was after a long-awaited success, but you felt emptier than ever.

People everywhere ponder the meaning of life, but they can't agree on the answer. Is life about love? Is it about having a nice car? Is it about having children? Is it about having a pet? Is it about having friends? Is it about working hard so you can enjoy the weekend? Is it about saving up for a nice retirement? Is it about vacations? Is it about money in the bank? Is it about making a contribution to society? Is it about world peace?

We spend most of our lives working furiously toward goals

that, when achieved, turn out to hold less substance than a Twinkie.

When it comes to the pursuit of happiness, the grass is always greener on the other side. So we obsess over fence hopping. We get degrees and start programs and change careers and become fans of Facebook causes because we know that happiness is just over the next fence.

To reference the deep intellectual thinker Weird Al Yankovic, we are like Harvey the Wonder Hamster. We spend our days on a hamster wheel, going nowhere frantically.

Life Is a Vapor

A few years ago, right around when I was stepping into my role as lead pastor, our church was rocked by several tragedies.

First, a much-loved pastor in our church named Aaron Haskins passed away in his sleep at the age of forty-nine. Aaron was one of the most likable people I have ever known, and he had been a dear friend of my family for fifteen years. He had a tremendous heart for people, and he was a champion for interracial unity in the Northwest. His death shocked us all.

My father passed away a year later, as I mentioned in the introduction. If you have lost a loved one, you understand my personal sense of loss. Wendell Smith was my hero, my mentor, and my best friend. He was larger than life: a man of unparalleled love, faith, and generosity. Now he was gone; our church was without its pastor, and I was without my dad.

Shortly after that, Aaron Haskins's son and namesake, Aaron Haskins, Jr., died suddenly in his sleep from heart

THE MEANING OF LIFE

failure. He was twenty-nine. Aaron had been my friend since childhood. Now his mother, Cheryl, was dealing with the loss of her husband and her son within eighteen months. Cheryl is my hero, by the way; her strength and wisdom in that impossible season were amazing.

Then a young woman in our church, a beautiful, talented, sweet-spirited musician named Carly, took her own life. She was a student at the University of Washington. She loved God and loved people. Her life seemed bright, which only made her death that much more bewildering.

Our church went through a number of other difficult circumstances in that period of time, not the least of which was the national housing crash and recession. I won't list all the tragedies, but we felt them all, and it was a struggle at times just to keep going.

As a church and as individuals, we were forced to consider the brevity of this life. It is a vapor: here and gone in a brief flash of time.

Was life about health? About family? We had prayed long and hard for my dad's healing, then he passed away. Was the point of religion just getting God to do what we wanted? Or could we find a way to grieve our loss without being shipwrecked in our faith?

Where is the meaning in your life? So you get the corner office. You get the bonus or promotion. You get that beautiful spouse, the person of your dreams. You get the child you've been asking God for. You move into that gorgeous house on a cul-de-sac that you've dreamed of for years. You buy your vacation home.

Is that really all there is to life?

JESUS IS _____.

Quoth the Raven

Possibly the strangest book in the Bible—certainly the most depressing—is the book of Ecclesiastes. It was written by Solomon, a king of Israel and the wisest man who ever lived. God allowed Solomon to have everything a person might want: bottomless wealth, worldwide fame, absolute power over a nation, hundreds of wives, and the wisdom to manage it all. It's a good thing he had wisdom, because with that many mothers-in-law, you could get yourself in hot water pretty quick. But that's another topic.

Solomon had all the gold, glory, and girls he could wish for. And then he writes Ecclesiastes, a rather disturbing book, where he meanders through all the meaningless things of life. As you read it, you start to wonder if his goal is to depress you. This guy would have gotten along well with Edgar Allan Poe and his dismal raven.

And yet, this book was included in the canon of Scripture. God wanted it there. It contains truth, and we could benefit from Solomon's wisdom.

Solomon was smart enough to look around and see how frantically everyone was pursuing happiness. This was several thousand years ago, but the human race hasn't changed that much. Yes, since then we've invented airplanes and toilet paper, but our psyche remains the same.

So Solomon decided to conduct a massive experiment in human happiness. He volunteered to be the test subject, conveniently enough. His goal, which he states at the beginning of the book, was to use his unbelievable resources to achieve happiness the way everyone around him was attempting to:

through power, fame, pleasure, and so on. He bought into the philosophy that you can't have too much of a good thing. If a little money, a little power, and a little sex felt good, a lot of it might be the ultimate source of meaning in life.

So here's this man who had everything any man would ever want, including the ability to think on a very high level. And as you read Ecclesiastes, you think, *Dude, what's wrong with this guy? Why isn't he happier?* His book chronicles how he systematically crashes and burns no matter what he tries. With each potential source of happiness, he notices that time and chance and death trump his efforts.

Here are the first two verses of the book: "These are the words of the Teacher, King David's son, who ruled in Jerusalem. 'Everything is meaningless,' says the Teacher, 'completely meaningless!'"

And that's the high point of the book. It pretty much goes downhill from there.

Solomon's cynicism targets, among other things:

1. Intelligence. "The greater my wisdom, the greater my grief. To increase knowledge only increases sorrow" (1:18).
2. Pleasure. "Anything I wanted, I would take. I denied myself no pleasure. I even found great pleasure in hard work, a reward for all my labors. But as I looked at everything I had worked so hard to accomplish, it was all so meaningless—like chasing the wind. There was nothing really worthwhile anywhere" (2:10–11).
3. Wisdom. "Yet I saw that the wise and the foolish share the same fate. Both will die. So I said to myself, 'Since I

will end up the same as the fool, what's the value of all my wisdom? This is all so meaningless!' For the wise and the foolish both die. The wise will not be remembered any longer than the fool. In the days to come, both will be forgotten" (2:14–16).

4. Work. "Some people work wisely with knowledge and skill, then must leave the fruit of their efforts to someone who hasn't worked for it. This, too, is meaningless, a great tragedy. So what do people get in this life for all their hard work and anxiety? Their days of labor are filled with pain and grief; even at night their minds cannot rest. It is all meaningless" (2:21–23).

5. Power. "Endless crowds stand around [the king], but then another generation grows up and rejects him, too. So it is all meaningless—like chasing the wind" (4:16–17).

6. Righteousness. "And this is not all that is meaningless in our world. In this life, good people are often treated as though they were wicked, and wicked people are often treated as though they were good. This is so meaningless!" (8:14).

7. Talent. "I have observed something else under the sun. The fastest runner doesn't always win the race, and the strongest warrior doesn't always win the battle. The wise sometimes go hungry, and the skillful are not necessarily wealthy. And those who are educated don't always lead successful lives. It is all decided by chance, by being in the right place at the right time" (9:11).

8. Education. "But, my child, let me give you some further advice: Be careful, for writing books is endless, and much study wears you out" (12:12).

Confessions of a Hamster

Solomon, the wisest man who ever lived, sums up the results of his experiment at the end of his book. "Let us hear the conclusion of the whole matter: Fear God and keep His commandments, for this is man's all" (12:13 NKJV).

It's safe to say that none of us will have access to the absolute wealth and power that Solomon had in his attempt to attain happiness.

But we keep trying.

At some point, we need to exit the hamster wheel and take an honest look at our lives. If we are not happy with the income we have now, or with our job, or with our marital status, we will never be happy. Those things cannot change an unhappy person into a happy person.

That's not to say the pleasures of life can't bring temporary happiness. Of course they can. Money can buy happiness. It's fun to buy new things—it just isn't the kind of happiness that lasts. Then we have to buy more things. Drugs and alcohol make us happy—for a few hours. Then we are left emptier than ever.

Ironically, the meaning of life is not found in this life. When Solomon said, "fear God and keep his commandments," he was saying that life is not about being happy. It's about God. Focusing on God brings meaning to our lives.

Fear does not mean terror. It means total awe. We should live in a state of awe at the magnificence, the beauty, and the majesty of the Creator of the universe. And in that state, we walk with him, we trust him, and we respond in love to him.

It's interesting that fearing God comes before keeping his

commandments. People who simply follow a list of laws are not in awe of God. They are bound by rules and regulations and duty. But when they fall in love with the awesomeness of God, and when they see his glory and his goodness, rules become secondary.

For many of us, that's a little ambiguous. Where is God? How do I see God? How can I be in awe of God?

God is not ambiguous. He is not ethereal or undefined. God reveals himself in Jesus. Jesus is the awesomeness of God, the glory of God, and the ultimate manifestation of God. He is God with skin on.

When we are in awe of Jesus, when we recognize his pre-eminence, we discover the meaning of life.

Some of us consider ourselves followers of Jesus, but we are experiencing a level of complexity and confusion that can be traced back to one thing: we have lost sight of the ultimate source of meaning in life.

When you are in awe of Jesus, it's amazing how uncomplicated marriage can be. It's amazing how uncomplicated running your business can be.

Life makes more sense when we don't make it about ourselves.

We tend to get distracted and disturbed over little things. They don't feel little, of course—they feel like matters of life and death. Like when you are having trouble with your boss, who is a shady, under-the-table sort of guy. And all of a sudden, the meaning of life is about being right. It's about you being promoted over your boss. You deserve the corner office, not him. And you get agitated and frustrated, and before you know it, you've lost the point of life. You think the point is proving your boss wrong and getting the corner office and doubling your income.

So, finally, you prove your boss wrong. He gets demoted, and you get promoted. You get the corner office. You are earning twice what you used to. But you will still sit in that corner office and find something to be upset about. Now, instead of the boss, it's the CEO you don't like. And the cycle continues.

If we really want to find what matters in this life, we will consider eternity. What matters most is what matters in eternity. And what matters in eternity is not income, or friendship, or fame, or pleasure. Those things are fine in themselves. God created them, and he loves to bless you with them. But they will not outlast death.

I love my wife. I love my kids. I even like my house, if you don't mind me saying so. But I cannot guarantee that they will be with me forever. Life is unpredictable and short. Time and life and chance have a way of messing with our plans. Solomon proved that very effectively.

You can take my stuff. You can take my position. You can even take my family. But you cannot take Jesus away from me. He is in my heart. His awesomeness, his majesty, his sufficiency, his love for me—those things will last for eternity. He is the ultimate meaning in this life and the life to come.

Focal Point

I enjoy interior design. Not the DIY kind, where you take classes in furniture restoration and deck building. Power tools and I have an agreement. I don't bother them and they don't bother me. When it comes to interior design, I like the BIY kind: buy it yourself.

In interior design, there is a concept sometimes referred to as the *focal point*. Every room has a focal point: an item, or a wall, or a corner that everything else points to. When people walk into the room, they consciously or unconsciously are drawn to that focal point.

Often, by default, the focal point is the television. Other times it's a piece of artwork. Or it's the view out a window. Or it's a giant stuffed elk head with beady glass eyes and eighteen-point antlers that you shot with a bow and arrow on a ten-day trek through the wilderness. Hey, that's not my thing, but I live in the Northwest, and you see stuff like that.

What is the focal point of our lives? Is it self? Is it our efforts? Is it our good deeds? Or is it Jesus?

If Jesus is the focal point of our lives, we don't live based on what is on the earth: what we can see, touch, feel, and sense. We don't have to be subject to the passions and philosophies that the world around us holds so dear. Instead, we orient and design our existence around heavenly truths and principles.

I don't pretend to be an expert in human psychology. If anything, I would be the guy on the couch, not the guy in the chair taking notes. But I am a feelings guy, and when my emotions are out of whack, I know it—and, unfortunately, so does everyone else. I've discovered when that happens, it's usually because I've forgotten what is important. I've lost sight of Jesus. I've let the pressures and disappointments of life hijack my thoughts.

Some of us sing songs every Sunday about how good and powerful God is. We tell him we surrender our lives to him.

Then we go to work on Monday and strive and stress as if it all depended on us. We make life about ourselves: about pleasing ourselves, about accomplishing our goals, about making things happen in our strength. It's a subtle, unspoken switch that flips in our minds from Sunday to Monday, but the results are plain: worry, depression, fear, anxiety, pride, anger, impatience, envy, bitterness, slander, confusion, and tension.

I don't know about you, but I prefer rest, peace, clarity, joy, and purpose. That's a list I can get excited about. Once Jesus is the focal point—once he is the culmination of life and the pinnacle of our existence—everything else makes sense. Life becomes simple again. Priorities fall into place, and peace, joy, and rest return.

"Come to me," Jesus calls to us today. "Come to me, all you who are weary and carry heavy burdens, and I will give you rest."

Jesus is the point of life.

JESUS IS happy.

NINE

Good News of Great Joy

The greatest thing about family is they are always there for you. Ironically, that is also the worst part. Christmas comes around, and so does the family. It's inevitable. You can run but you cannot hide. I don't mean any disrespect, but I'm sure you can relate.

How can family be so blissful and so painful at the same time? How can they be so loyal and yet so . . . weird?

I'm not talking about my family, of course, since most of them will read this book. I'm talking about yours. I'm just trying to feel your pain.

Families are loud. Families invade your personal space. Families tell you that you've put on weight since they last saw you. Families smell like pretzels. Families eat the last piece of leftover pie, the one you hid under a paper plate in the fridge. Families think it's cute when their kid beats up your kid. "Ah, he gave him a bloody nose. So cute. Well, you know, boys will be boys."

For your reading enjoyment, I've gathered some quotes on family from a few of my favorite theologians. I found them online so I know they are legit, because everything you read on the Internet is true.

The first is by theologian George Burns: "Happiness is having a large, caring, close-knit family in another city."

This is my favorite, by theologian Jeff Foxworthy: "If you ever start feeling like you have the goofiest, craziest, most dysfunctional family in the world, all you have to do is go to a state fair, because five minutes at the fair, you'll be going, 'You know what? We're all right. We are dang near royalty.'"

And finally, pastor Jerry Seinfeld says, "There is no such thing as fun for the whole family."

I swear that's in Proverbs somewhere.

Sand Castles

I don't mean to pick on family. Family is wonderful. Family gives us a place to belong, an identity, a sense of value. Our family loves us no matter what. They encourage us and believe in us. When done right, I think it is the greatest source of joy this side of heaven. But ultimately, our family is not the key to our happiness.

Some people tie their emotional stability—or lack thereof—to family. If they aren't happy, they think it's because they come from a bad family, or because they don't have a family, or because they have a bad marriage or bad kids. If their family would just get their act together, they would be happy.

We do the same thing in other areas of life. We think, *If I just had that career, I would be happy.* Or, *If I could just make that much money each year, I would be happy.*

All of us are pursuing happiness and joy. No matter what each of us believes about God or life after death, we all want happiness and joy. It is one of the ultimate goals of man. Thomas Jefferson famously called the pursuit of happiness an "inalienable right" given to us by our Creator.

Desiring happiness, peace, and joy is not wrong. But how we pursue them is important. For example, my right to happiness cannot involve depriving you of your right to happiness. You've probably heard the expression, "The right to swing my fist ends where the other man's nose begins."

Most of us are decent enough people to not stomp on everyone else just to be happy. Our real problem is that we search for satisfaction in the wrong places. And we come up empty. So, like Solomon in Ecclesiastes, we become disillusioned with life.

Happiness is really not as elusive as people think. But we have to start with the right perspective. We have to realize, as we discussed in the previous chapter, that Jesus is the point of life.

Here's a truth that could change your life: *true happiness cannot be found in anything unless it is first found in God.*

Family cannot bring us happiness. Packages on our doorstep cannot bring us happiness. Seeing our names in lights cannot bring us happiness. Landing that big contract will not bring us happiness. A new car, a new drill, a new coffeemaker— big or small, nothing on this earth can bring true happiness unless we first find joy in God.

Trying to find happiness of the soul by grasping at the little pleasures of life is like trying to build a sandcastle in an inch of water. The harder you work and the faster you scramble, the more things cave in around you.

God wants you to be happy, but joy has to be first found in God. Joy has to be first found in the good news of Jesus Christ. And when joy is found there, you'll find joy in everything else.

Jesus and Joy

People often read Luke 2:1–20 at Christmas because it tells the story of Jesus's birth. There is a little phrase in this story that says a lot about the nature of God and the gospel. Here is the entire passage:

At that time the Roman emperor, Augustus, decreed that a census should be taken throughout the Roman Empire. (This was the first census taken when Quirinius was governor of Syria.) All returned to their own ancestral towns to register for this census. And because Joseph was a descendant of King David, he had to go to Bethlehem in Judea, David's ancient home. He traveled there from the village of Nazareth in Galilee. He took with him Mary, his fiancée, who was now obviously pregnant.

And while they were there, the time came for her baby to be born. She gave birth to her first child, a son. She wrapped him snugly in strips of cloth and laid him in a manger, because there was no lodging available for them.

That night there were shepherds staying in the fields nearby, guarding their flocks of sheep. Suddenly, an angel of the Lord appeared among them, and the radiance of the

Lord's glory surrounded them. They were terrified, but the angel reassured them. "Don't be afraid!" he said. "I bring you good news that will bring great joy to all people. The Savior—yes, the Messiah, the Lord—has been born today in Bethlehem, the city of David! And you will recognize him by this sign: You will find a baby wrapped snugly in strips of cloth, lying in a manger."

Suddenly, the angel was joined by a vast host of others—the armies of heaven—praising God and saying,

"Glory to God in highest heaven,
and peace on earth to those with whom God is
pleased."

When the angels had returned to heaven, the shepherds said to each other, "Let's go to Bethlehem! Let's see this thing that has happened, which the Lord has told us about."

They hurried to the village and found Mary and Joseph. And there was the baby, lying in the manger. After seeing him, the shepherds told everyone what had happened and what the angel had said to them about this child. All who heard the shepherds' story were astonished, but Mary kept all these things in her heart and thought about them often. The shepherds went back to their flocks, glorifying and praising God for all they had heard and seen. It was just as the angel had told them.

The phrase that stands out to me was spoken by the angel who announced Jesus's birth to the shepherds. He said, "I bring you good news that will bring great joy to all people."

Jesus and joy are always a package deal. And it's not just your average joy—it's great joy.

"Good news" is the English translation of the Greek word *euangelion*. (The New Testament was originally written in Greek.) This Greek word is also translated *gospel* or *preach*, and it is the root of the word *evangelism*.

In other words, the gospel is by nature good news. *Gospel* and *good news* are synonyms. The gospel is not bad news. It's not threatening news. It's not hellfire-and-brimstone news. It's good news. Great news. Over-the-moon news. You cannot separate joy from the gospel. Joy is built into the very definition of the gospel. They are literally the same word.

The answer to your happiness problem is not taking a vacation, reading a joke book, getting a nap, or listening to a comedian. The answer to your joy problem is the gospel.

Jesus Laughing

Some people can't understand how God and happiness could go together. They think religion and fun are fundamentally opposed. To them, God is a cosmic party pooper. A grinch. A fun sponge. A spoilsport. God is against parties and fun and pleasure, so God is the antithesis of happiness.

Nothing could be further from the truth. God invented happiness. He came up with the concept of humor. He created our ability to have fun. He built a beautiful world and gave us five senses to enjoy it. Our pleasure gives him pleasure. If we love to be happy, and if we were created in his image, then how much more does God radiate joy?

Jesus is happy. I don't know what's wrong with many of the paintings and movies about Jesus, but for some reason he looks like a zombie half the time. His eyes are freaky and he never smiles. He looks stressed out or high on drugs or something.

That wasn't Jesus. Do you know how I know? Because kids liked to be with him. Kids don't like creepy people. They don't like grumpy people. Yet Jesus had so many kids wanting to come to him that his disciples felt they had to forbid it.

The Bible says about Jesus, "You love justice and hate evil. Therefore, O God, your God has anointed you, pouring out the oil of joy on you more than on anyone else" (Hebrews 1:9). Jesus was the happiest guy around. He told jokes. He poked fun at people. He laughed.

For some people, the thought of Jesus laughing seems irreverent, like happiness means he wasn't holy or something. There is a statement I've heard that I take issue with: "God is more concerned with our holiness than our happiness." I think holiness is the key to happiness, and I think happiness can be the purest expression of holiness. Really, you can't separate the two.

The Bible is full of words like *joy, rejoice, blessing, happiness,* and *peace.* Happiness is a natural result of knowing God and of experiencing his love. Time and time again, when the Bible describes what it means to be a true follower of God, it uses the word *blessed.* That term can be translated *happy* or *pleased.* Authentic faith produces happiness, pleasure, enjoyment, and blessing.

Happy Feet

There is a poetic passage in Isaiah 52:7 that says, "How beautiful on the mountains are the feet of the messenger who brings good news, the good news of peace and salvation, the news that the God of Israel reigns!" This verse talks about how wonderful it is to be the person who carries good news to people who need to hear it. Messengers with good news have beautiful feet. They have happy feet.

Most people reading this book are probably not pastors, but since I am, I'm going to pick on my own species for a minute. I was studying the passage I quoted from Luke 2 in preparation for a Christmas message a couple of years ago, and suddenly it hit me: my primary purpose as a preacher is to declare good news, news that produces great joy in people.

It was a paradigm shift. Not that I would stand in the pulpit and scream at people before that—I'm a nice guy—but I think I was afraid of preaching too good of a gospel.

Sometimes preachers feel that we have to balance the good news and the bad news. We try to offset the really good passages with something more ominous.

I'd better not make it too good, now, because people will abuse it, we think. *People will misuse it. People will misunderstand it. If I tell them that God has finished the work, that he has redeemed and accepted them, that he loves them and is not mad at them, that he forgives all sin, past, present, or future, they might start acting crazy. I'd better keep it balanced.*

Then we start preaching, and we wax eloquent about the goriness of sin and the sneakiness of the devil, and we run out of time before we get to the good news. So we try to squeeze it in during our closing prayer, but by then it's too late.

It's sort of like doing the good cop, bad cop routine, only we play both parts. Our congregation doesn't know what to expect from their bipolar pastor when they show up. Last week the sermon was about love and grace, and this week it's about fire and fear and foul spirits. And our people are thinking, *Wow. Guess somebody woke up on the wrong side of the bed today.* If they invited a new person this week, they apologize. "He's not always like this. Usually he's funnier. And . . . happier." And they determine to pray for their pastor because he's clearly under a lot of stress.

Understanding that the gospel is good news should help us all be a little more cheerful, a little nicer to hang out with. Preaching and evangelizing are nothing more than sharing good news with people. Some of us are passionate about telling people about Jesus, but we freak them out because we never learned how to smile. We dangle them over hell and then wonder why they don't want anything to do with our gospel. If you say you preach the gospel but there is no great joy, I'd say there is a problem with your gospel.

I don't want to be a person who cares more about whether a guy smokes or does drugs than whether he feels loved. I don't want to be a pastor who preaches love and acceptance but avoids the teenage gang member who hangs around outside the church. I don't want to belong to a church that treats a woman differently because she happens to walk into church in a dress that shows off a little too much skin. You know, cleavage does not intimidate God. Smoke that, religion. Maybe that's the only "nice" dress she owns. Maybe everyone she knows dresses that way. Maybe she's desperate, and she's thinking that if she doesn't find some authentic love and joy today, she might end it all.

I'm not advocating sloppiness or sensuality in church, but I am advocating a church that reflects real life, a church where real people with real problems can come and find hope and joy. I want people in my church to welcome everybody: the gay, the straight, the rich, the poor, the good, the bad, and the ugly. I want my church to be a place where people can come in from all kinds of backgrounds and issues and short-comings and addictions and bondages, and we don't have to get them all fixed up before they sit on the front row.

That's the gospel. It's good news for everyone. It's not good news just for people who are already good, for those who are self-controlled and disciplined enough to have all their ducks in a row. It's good news for the people who can't even find their ducks. They haven't seen some of their ducks in years. Their lives are a mess. But they can come to Jesus and find instant acceptance. They belong long before they believe and long before they behave.

"Man, I don't belong here."

"Sure you do."

"No, look, everyone's dressed up all nice."

"That's just how they feel comfortable. They won't care how you dress. They won't even notice."

"I need to go out for a smoke."

"No problem, I'll save your seat."

"Can my partner and I come to your church? Do we belong?"

"Of course! Sit up here with me. You're among friends."

For some of us, there's a little voice inside asking, *So, when are you going to lead your friend to Jesus? He needs to get saved!*

Here's a tip. Jesus is really good at saving people. I'm not. So I'm going to let him do that, if you don't mind. I'm going to just make sure my friend knows he belongs.

Don't get me wrong. I'm not saying that we should never tell people about Jesus. Actually, I'm convinced that when we grasp the goodness of God, when we are full of the joy of his salvation, we won't be able to keep our mouths shut. We will tell them about Jesus because he has changed our lives. We will tell them about Jesus out of genuine love and compassion, because we know that without Jesus we would be in the same boat, and we want them to experience the happiness we have found.

That is way more appealing to people than force-feeding them salvation because we feel guilty about their eternal destinies.

Sometimes our approach reminds me of that profound, cinematic masterpiece *Nacho Libre.*

> **NACHO:** "I'm a little concerned right now about your salvation and stuff. How come you have not been baptized?"

> **ESQUELETO:** "Because I never got around to it, okay? I don't know why you always have to be judging me because I only believe in science."

And we sneak up behind them and dunk their heads in a bowl, and we feel better about ourselves. We did our religious duty. But they haven't changed. They haven't met Jesus. They haven't met joy.

Bad News Bears

It's not just preachers who focus on bad news more than good news. Turn on the local newscast; bad news abounds in our culture and society. When it comes to life in general, we are used to bad news. We are comfortable with bad news. Many of us expect bad news. I've met sickos who seem to relish bad news. They look for the cloud around every silver lining. If your joy level is low, ask yourself what kind of news you are listening to.

God is counterculture. God brings good news. The angel's announcement to those shepherds was the greatest good news this planet had ever heard. The shepherds figured that out. That's why they were pumped out of their minds.

It's human nature to mistrust what seems too good to be true. Let's settle in our hearts once and for all that Jesus is too good to be true. Salvation is too good to be true. Grace is too good to be true. Heaven is too good to be true.

One of the greatest indictments against Christians is not sin or hypocrisy. It's our lack of joy. Something is wrong when we call ourselves Christians but we practically have an aneurysm just trying to crack a smile.

Some people take themselves too seriously. They take everything too seriously. They take their hair too seriously. They take flossing too seriously. They take their spouse's mistakes too seriously. They take their schoolwork too seriously.

They even take jokes too seriously. Have you ever had someone tell you a joke and they're like, "Oh, I . . . I can't . . . that's not . . . I messed up the punch line. I just totally ruined that. I'm terrible at jokes. Why do I do this? Oh, my God. What's my problem? I'm just—I just totally ruined the joke. I'm sorry."

Dude, it's a joke! Don't take it so seriously.

Some people take their past too seriously. They take their present too seriously. They take their future too seriously.

We can get too serious about life, and it actually reflects poorly on the gospel, because the gospel, by definition, is good news. There's nothing bad or sad about God's gospel. It is only good news.

Think about it. If I preached about love, joy, and happiness from the pulpit, but my kids always walked around sad and dejected, never looking people in the eyes, never talking to anyone—at some point, people would wonder what was wrong with me. My kids' attitudes are a direct reflection of me as a parent.

There are people who think walking around with a long face and reciting a list of their sufferings makes them more spiritual, but it doesn't. It just makes them unpleasant to be around. It certainly doesn't make people want to hear what they have to say about God.

I preach good news, and I'm not going to apologize for that. The good news about Jesus produces joy in the hearts of people. It replaces depression, condemnation, and hopelessness with joy, faith, and hope.

"I bring you good news that will bring great joy to all people." That's the gospel. Joy is central. Joy is imperative.

Joy of the Lord

The Bible says in Nehemiah 8:10, "Don't be dejected and sad, for the joy of the Lord is your strength!" It doesn't say exercise is your strength, or hard work is your strength, or winning the lottery is your strength. It doesn't even say joy is your strength. It's the joy that comes from the Lord that is our strength.

Some of us are weary, and we think maybe it's because we're overworked or because we're not getting enough sleep. So we take sleeping pills and buy mattresses intelligent enough to have a measurable IQ, and we try to get some rest. And yet, we still feel lethargic. Our strength seems zapped.

The problem isn't a lack of sleep; it's a lack of joy. Our strength is connected to our joy, and our joy is connected to the gospel we believe in.

I'm not promoting fake joy, the smile-for-the-camera kind of joy that doesn't make it past your Botox. It's not about forcing laughter and bubbly words just so you'll look spiritual.

"Well, I read this book that says I have to be joyful. Because, you know, joy is part of the gospel. And I want to look like someone who believes the gospel, and if I don't smile a lot, it makes God look bad." So we laugh and smile and high-five everyone, but at home we're grouchier than ogres with hemorrhoids.

The joy of the Lord is authentic. It seeps into the core of who we are and holds us in a perpetual state of peace and happiness. The joy of the Lord strengthens us, soothes us, and sustains us.

True happiness is a state of being, not just a passing emotion. Even when external circumstances rock our emotions for a time, we are able to strengthen ourselves by trusting in the Lord.

David prayed this prayer, recorded in Psalm 51: "Restore to me the joy of Your salvation." A lot of times it gets misquoted as "Restore to me the joy of my salvation." It's not my salvation—it's God's. I am not the originator or the creator. It's his work of grace. It's his initiative.

There is a perpetual state of joy that comes with the

gospel. No matter what we are going through, no matter what circumstances we are facing right now, when we understand the gospel, it will keep us in a state of happiness and joy.

The gospel and joy are a package deal. It's the original Happy Meal. The box reads, "Free joy inside. No assembly required."

It's God's grace, God's joy, and God's strength, and we have free and complete access to it. It doesn't get better than that.

TEN

With Us and For Us

Bubba Watson is one of my good friends. We've known each other for several years now. I like golf, and since Bubba is a tolerably good golfer, we've played quite a few games together.

In case you missed it, Bubba won the 2012 Masters Golf Tournament. I just checked and he is currently the fourth-ranked golfer in the world. That means out of six billion people on the planet, he's number four. In America, he's number one.

When we've played together, Bubba or I have often brought friends along. As you can imagine, many of them get incredibly nervous. I get a kick out of watching it. I'm sick like that.

The big reason they get nervous is they feel like they need to impress Bubba with their golf game. That, of course, is laughable. Whatever you can do on the golf course, I guarantee Bubba can do better. Your little golf ball, even on the longest, straightest drive of your life, is going to be sitting in the middle of the fairway, waving at Bubba's ball as it flies overhead and lands a hundred and fifty yards farther down the fairway.

I tell my friends to relax. You can't impress Bubba with your golf skills. It's not going to happen. And by the way, Bubba is not critiquing your golf game. He's a bigger man than that. So just have fun. Enjoy the game. Relish the experience. Laugh at your mistakes because they don't matter.

I've noticed I sometimes try to impress God. That's funny, because my goodness is even more laughable than my golf game.

Do we think we can impress God with our love, our righteous acts, our amazing sacrifices? Is God going to leap to his feet in heaven and say, "Oh my goodness, angels, did you see that? Did someone get that on camera? Not even my Son can do that! Wow!"

We spend so much time trying to pay God back, to impress him. "See, God, see? See what I did? Do you love me more now? Will you answer more of my prayers now?"

News flash—whatever you can do, Jesus can do better.

There is only one person God is impressed with, and that is Jesus. If you want to impress God, trust in Jesus. When you trust in Jesus, your life is hidden in Christ. It's wrapped up in Jesus. When God looks at you, he sees his Son. That's when he says, "Wow!"

God is not critiquing our performance. He is not judging our behavior. He is not cataloging our sins for future reference. That was all done away with when we put our faith in Jesus. That's good news, because now we can enjoy life. Jesus did—and he was happy. Sure, there were moments when he was sad, but even in his sadness he had an unshakeable confidence in the love of the Father.

Belong, Believe, Behave

One of the reasons the gospel is so good is that it's more about God than about us. That's good news, because God is a lot more trustworthy than we are.

Part of our problem is that we think about ourselves way too much. The more we obsess about our problems, our weaknesses, and our deficiencies, the more we perpetuate them. It's ironic but true.

The gospel is not seventeen steps to reaching God. That would be bad news, because we would figure out how to mess it up.

The gospel is God reaching us. That's why it's really good news. The amazing thing is that when we focus on his goodness, his power, and his grace, those seventeen things start to happen in our lives, all on their own. We are hardly even aware of what is happening, but the results are obvious. We begin to change; we begin to be more like Jesus.

The gospel is the opposite of religion, at least religion as many people live it. Religion says that obedience brings acceptance. The gospel teaches the opposite: acceptance brings obedience.

Religion says: "Behave, believe, and then you will belong." That's the order many of us have known our whole lives. "First I have to act right, think right, and talk right, then I'll fit in. Then I'll belong."

The gospel says the opposite: "Belong, then believe, then behave." Another way of saying that is: "Amazing grace, great faith, and good works."

Ephesians 2:8–10 states: "For by grace you have been saved

through faith, and that not of yourselves; it is the gift of God, not of works, lest anyone should boast. For we are His workmanship, created in Christ Jesus for good works, which God prepared beforehand that we should walk in them" (NKJV).

Notice the divine order. First comes grace, then comes belief, then comes good works. Many of us get that switched up in our minds. We think our good works come first. We have to impress God so he will accept us. We have to deserve God. So we obsess over our spiritual résumés and we try to show the God who invented quantum physics how smart we are.

Many of us have fallen for this philosophy we call the gospel, but really it is religion. It is empty works. And we think, *Great joy? About what? The gospel is just a lot of work.*

We still live on the basis that because I obey, I am accepted. There is no joy in that. There is certainly no amazement in that. What is amazing about the idea that I am accepted because I behave? That is normal human thinking. That is how society and culture work. No wonder there is no great joy connected to the gospel we say we believe in.

Some of us treat life as if it is a qualifying round for the Pro-Am Heaven Golf Tournament. If we can play well enough, if we can impress the Big Man with our technique and our execution, if we can do better than most other Christians, we will make it into heaven. But of course we triple bogey on the first hole, then we spend the next seventeen holes mad at ourselves for messing up.

God doesn't want us to make life about our amateur efforts at holiness. He wants us to enjoy life. We only get one, after all. Sin tried to ruin it and the devil tried to steal it, but God came down of his own initiative, in his own power, on the basis of his own righteousness, motivated by his own love, and he saved us. That's good news! If that doesn't get you excited, you better start shopping for a casket, because you might be dead.

Happy and Holy

All of this is not to say we should continue in sin. Why would we even want to? Why would we intentionally disappoint the one who loves us the most? How ridiculous would it be to sin on purpose, knowing that sin cost Jesus his life, that it brings pain and death, and that it sabotages the happy, blessed life God created for us?

God's commandments are all motivated by his desire for our happiness, by his desire to protect us and bless us. Even his correction and his rebukes are proof of his love.

When we follow the true gospel, even God's commands and restrictions bring joy to our hearts. They show us the path of life. They teach us to avoid traps. They give us wisdom.

When we stop being insecure about our performance and instead trust in Jesus's finished work, we are free to live a new kind of holiness. It's a holiness that is internally motivated, a holiness powered by love, not by guilt. "Loving God means keeping his commandments, and his commandments are not burdensome," the apostle John wrote. "For every child of God defeats this evil world, and we achieve this victory through our faith" (1 John 5:3–4).

It's incredible, really—when we let Jesus love us and learn to love him in return, holiness happens. But when we fixate on our sin . . . that other stuff happens. You know what I mean. I read it on your bumper sticker.

I think *sour Christian* should be a contradiction in terms. As I stated earlier, holiness results in happiness, and happiness is an expression of holiness. The two go together. I am happier because I am holy, and it's easier to be holier because I am happy. Because of the good news, because of Jesus, I can be both holy and happy—what a concept!

Are You Talking to Us?

The gospel is good news because it can be summed up in the phrase "God with us." Matthew 1:23 quotes a prophetic passage from the Old Testament: "Look! The virgin will conceive a child! She will give birth to a son, and they will call him Immanuel, which means 'God is with us.'"

That is the gospel: God is with us. Jesus is God in the flesh, here on earth, hanging out with sinful people.

It's fascinating that the first people who hear about Jesus's birth are shepherds. Because of the nature of their job, shepherds were incapable of fulfilling parts of the religious ceremonial law, including the rigorous hand washings. Shepherds were actually despised by the religious people of the day because they could never completely fulfill the law.

The angel came to those who couldn't fulfill the law and told them that someone has come who will fulfill the law for them.

"Us? Are you talking to us?" the shepherds must have asked the angel.

"Yeah, to you, you lawbreaker. This child is born unto you. He is a gift to you. He is for you. He is with you."

No wonder these shepherds were so excited. They were thinking, *Was this a mistake? I bet they meant to go to the house of one of the rabbis. Maybe their GPS malfunctioned or something. We don't even keep the law—why are they coming to us?*

To truly appreciate the significance of this phrase "God is with us," you have to understand that they lived in a time period when God was not readily available. But now, suddenly, he was among them. A holy, righteous, perfect, just God had come down to live with sinners, with people who could not fulfill the law. They could see him, they could hear him, they could touch him. He was with them.

Even though Jesus is in heaven now, we live under a new covenant, a new arrangement between God and man that Jesus instituted through his death and resurrection. We don't live under the law, which kept God and man separate. The new covenant that Jesus instituted says that God will always be with us. It's his promise to mankind. He is always available to us.

That's the good news of the gospel.

JESUS IS <u>here</u>.

ELEVEN

The One You Love

Have you ever, in the heat of the moment, said something that you later regretted?

Chelsea and I got married twelve years ago. A few months prior, we went through premarital counseling, which is supposed to prepare you for marriage. As if anything could prepare you for marriage.

By the way, my favorite question to ask engaged couples is "Are you ready to get married?" Typically, the guy opens his mouth and says, "Yeah!" And you know for sure he is most certainly not ready.

But in an attempt to be ready for marriage, Chelsea and I read a book called *The Five Love Languages* by Dr. Gary Chapman. It was very helpful.

Dr. Chapman says every person has one or more "love languages." We show our love for others using these languages, and we also feel loved when other people use the language we prefer. The five are: acts of service, words of affirmation, gifts, physical touch, and quality time.

Everyone has a top love language, says this book, and then we have maybe a top three. My top three go like this: words of affirmation, touch, and then touch me again. I bet some men can relate.

Growing up, I was very influenced by my mom and my older sister. My mom's top three love languages are acts of service, acts of service, and acts of service. No question. My sister is also very easy to figure out: it's gifts, gifts, and gifts. Since these were the women I grew up around, I started to think, *That's what women like: acts of service and gifts.*

The Five Love Languages also says, and it seems true to me, that we tend to dispense the kind of love we desire. So here I am in the first year or so of our marriage, just pouring on words of affirmation. And I'm trying to touch my wife, you know, and we're playing tag. And I'm giving her gifts and I'm buying her things, and it doesn't seem to be resonating.

One afternoon, things came to a head.

I came home, and I must have been playing golf or something. I'd had a good round, and I was thinking, *This is going to be a great night. We're going to make dinner, then we're going to make something else, and it's going to be a great night.*

So I walk into the house and I immediately notice that Chelsea seems a bit distant, a bit put off. And finally, I start asking, "Babe, is anything wrong? What's wrong?"

"No, nothing's wrong. Nothing."

Now, when a woman says nothing is wrong, it means everything is wrong, but she just doesn't know where to start. I've found that out the hard way, so trust me.

"Nothing."

Yeah, right.

So I keep pressing. "No, babe—honestly, what's wrong?"

Things start to escalate. She's so emotional. I'm reasonably stable, you know, but she just loses her emotions. Okay, maybe it's the other way around.

I keep prying. My voice might have entered another octave. "I mean, come on. What did I do? What did I do?"

"It's not what you did."

Now I'm like, *What? So it's who I am?* And I'm so confused. It's like she's giving me signals, and I'm not figuring them out. I'm getting more and more frustrated, until finally she just spells it out for me, because I'm a guy and I need that.

"I just, I just feel like we don't get enough time together."

"What do you mean? We're together right now. We sleep together. We live together. We eat together. I mean, what more do you want?"

"We don't get enough real time together."

That's when, in the heat of the moment, it came out. I don't know if I meant to say it, but it just slipped out.

Fast-forward for a minute. Recently, I was preparing a message and I told Chelsea, "I need an illustration of when I said something in the heat of the moment that I regretted."

Without hesitation, she goes, "Oh, I know! I know just the one. Why don't you tell the church about that time twelve years ago, when we were in the living room of our house, and you said, 'Why can't you have any other love language than quality time?' Tell them that."

"My God, woman, get healing! You need counseling. That was twelve years ago. I'm a better man."

Which means, "I don't say things like that anymore. I just think them."

Just kidding.

Not really.

Back to our newlywed experience. "We don't get enough real time together," my bride says.

"Really?" I'm exasperated by now. I mean, my emotions are at a high. "Really? Can't you have any other love language than quality time? Be like my sister—you give her a gift, and you don't have to spend time with her for three months. How awesome is that?"

It didn't go over very well. I'm still paying for that one.

Maybe you've done it too. You're in the heat of the moment, and you don't mean to, but something wells up inside, and you blurt it out. The Bible says that out of the abundance of the heart, the mouth speaks. Sigmund Freud said the same thing, but he used bigger words, and now we call it a Freudian slip.

When you're in the heat of the moment, typically what you really believe comes out. What you really want to say slips out, and you can't get it back. It can be painful or embarrassing, but it can also be revealing.

The One You Love

In John 11, we find a moving story about three siblings: Martha, Mary, and Lazarus. Most scholars believe Martha was the oldest sibling, Mary was the middle, and Lazarus was the little brother. Interestingly, Lazarus was never recorded as saying one word in Scripture. Apparently his big sisters said it all. Poor guy.

In this passage, Mary and Martha are in the heat of the

moment. Their little brother's life is on the line. The Bible puts it this way:

> Now, a certain man was sick, Lazarus of Bethany, the town of Mary and her sister Martha. It was that Mary who anointed the Lord with fragrant oil and wiped His feet with her hair, whose brother Lazarus was sick.
>
> Therefore, the sisters sent to Him saying, "Lord, behold, he whom You love is sick."
>
> When Jesus heard that, He said, "This sickness is not unto death, but for the glory of God, that the Son of God may be glorified through it." Now, Jesus loved Martha and her sister and Lazarus. (John 11:1–5 NKJV)

Besides his disciples, Martha, Mary, and Lazarus were perhaps Jesus's best friends. Jesus loved them deeply.

The fact that Jesus had friends at all might surprise a few people who think he floated around two feet off the ground and only had time for healing people and preaching. He was a normal-looking and normal-acting guy. Except he healed the sick, raised the dead, and never sinned. And he was God. Minor details.

In this story, Lazarus is hours from death. He is on the doorstep of death. And Mary and Martha, true to form, are speaking on Lazarus's behalf. They need to get God's attention. They have one shot at convincing Jesus to come. They need to come up with their best argument, their most airtight appeal. So they write Jesus a note. It has to be a good one—their brother's life depends on it.

It's the heat of the moment, and they aren't thinking about

being polite and courteous and wordy. What they really believe is about to be revealed. How are they going to appeal to Jesus? What will their plea be?

Now, if we were Lazarus's siblings, a lot of us would have started out by listing all the good things Lazarus had done. We would have talked about how much he loved and admired Jesus and how he was a model citizen who didn't deserve to die.

Not Mary and Martha.

They knew what moved Jesus.

"Lord, the one that *you love* is sick."

That was the realization that welled up from deep within their hearts. Jesus loved Lazarus.

It wasn't their love for Jesus, or Lazarus's love, or his good deeds that moved Jesus. It was pointless to recite a laundry list of their brother's achievements. That wasn't what moved the heart of Jesus. It was his own love that motivated him. It was his own desire to bless and heal and restore.

The story goes on to say that Jesus responded to Mary and Martha's request and went to their home. But by the time he arrived, Lazarus had died. That didn't bother Jesus—he knew it was going to happen. He simply raised Lazarus from the dead. It pays to have friends like that.

John, one of Jesus's disciples, recorded this story. John understood the importance of Jesus's love. Five times in his book, John calls himself "the disciple whom Jesus loved." He doesn't even use his own name. He just flaunts that he was Jesus's favorite.

Was he Jesus's favorite? We don't know. It doesn't really matter, because he believed he was. And there is something strangely healthy about that perspective. We are all God's favorites.

Some might call John's statements arrogant, but John didn't care. Neither did God, apparently—it's in his book. John defined his identity through Jesus's love. I find that fascinating.

A few decades later, John wrote several letters that are also part of the Bible. The letters are manifestos of God's love toward us. Here's one example from 1 John 4:9–10:

> God showed how much he loved us by sending his one and only Son into the world so that we might have eternal life through him. This is real love—not that we loved God, but that he loved us and sent his Son as a sacrifice to take away our sins.

John figured something out by watching Jesus. It's not about how much we love God. It's about how much he loves us.

That little truth will change the way you think, the way you talk, and the way you pray. For too many of us, life is all about how much we can accomplish. It's about our plans, our work, our merit, our achievements. That's gratifying to the ego, but ultimately it's a dead end. We find ourselves in situations we can't get out of, in need of favors we don't deserve. We lose our perspective very quickly when we make life all about us.

Mary and Martha were some of Jesus's closest friends. John, according to scholars, was probably Jesus's closest disciple. It seems the people nearest Jesus had an overwhelming awareness of his love for them. Maybe we should take a hint.

Let Me Count the Ways

The message Mary and Martha sent was a plea, a prayer. And notice the basis of their prayer: "the one you love."

You can find out a lot about what you really believe when you listen to yourself pray, when you listen to what you say in the heat of the moment. How many times have I prayed prayers like this: "Oh, God, I need help. I'm faithful. I help people. I'm generous. I'm holy. I read my Bible. And I'm praying really, really loudly, with big words and Bible verses and lots of praise. So come, Lord, and help me with my need."

In other words, "Lord, based on what I've done, now please do . . ." We think that moves God. No, what moves God is his Son. What moves God is his love.

One of the most famous love poems of all time, Elizabeth Barrett Browning's Sonnet 43, starts out: "How do I love thee? Let me count the ways."

Don't count the ways you love God; count the ways he loves you. Your love pales in comparison to his. So when you pray, pray like Mary and Martha: "Jesus, the one you love needs you."

I was tired the other afternoon, for instance. Maybe not a big deal, but I had some things I had to accomplish that evening, and I really needed strength. So, I got alone for a few minutes, and I said, "Lord, the one you love is tired. Give me energy."

It was such a refreshing, healthy way to pray. It was incredible. I started thinking, *Whoa. That was crazy. That felt good.*

He's moved by his love. Remind him of his love for you.

"Lord, the one you love is out $250 this month. I can't pay the bills. But I'm your favorite. I'm the one you love, so help me with my bills, Lord."

That's far better than trying to talk God into something based on our own works or our own merit.

Maybe you are thinking, *I don't really know Jesus. I'm a poor excuse for a follower of Jesus.*

Nobody's an outsider when we pray this way. It's on the basis of his love, not ours. We have no idea how profound his love for us really is. No matter who you are, no matter what you need, try praying that prayer. And I pray that your heart erupts with an understanding and revelation of his amazing love for you.

"God, because I am the object of your obsession, because I'm the one you love, come now and take care of my needs."

What is the focus of the Bible? Man loving God, or God loving man?

Many of us would answer automatically, "It's about man loving God. It's about humans leaving a sinful lifestyle and turning to God." And even if we didn't say it, we believe it—just look at how we pray and how we act.

We would be wrong.

All sixty-six books of the Bible, all forty-plus authors writing over the course of sixteen hundred years, point to the same thing: God's love for humanity.

If you're like me, you find yourself time and time again obsessing over your own inconsistencies and inadequacies, over your own love or lack of love for God. But if we spent more time in the Bible, we would discover that it is overwhelmingly about God's love for us. In fact, God's love created our love.

Here's a crazy thought: God's love is so extravagant and so inexplicable that he loved us before we were us. He loved us before we existed. He knew many of us would reject him, hate him, curse him, rebel against him. Yet he chose to love us. God loves us because he is love.

The message is clear in Scripture. The gospel is about God loving man, whether we reciprocate it or not. John, the "one Jesus loved," spelled it out: "We love Him because He first loved us" (1 John 4:19 NKJV).

The reason that we are even interested in God is that he is hot on our trails. We are his favorites, and he is passionately pursuing us. He doesn't just love us like a friend, like an aunt or uncle, or even like a dad. His love is far more perfect than any earthly love.

Really, we won't fully comprehend his love until we enter eternity with him. And when we get to eternity, we will be undone. We will be overwhelmed and overcome and consumed with the enormity of his love.

Picture that the next time you pray, the next time you fail at something, the next time you are facing a tough situation—it will revolutionize everything.

Go ahead and try to describe the height of his love, the length of his love, the width of his love, the depth of his love. Our metaphors pale in comparison. We have marriages, we have children, we have adoptions, we have friends, but nothing compares to God's love for us.

I've never met a person who exaggerated God's love. Never. It's impossible. He loved us first, he loves us best, and he will love us forever.

How does he love me?

I'll spend the rest of my life counting the ways.

TWELVE

It Is Well

People's last words are usually significant. Whether they are leaving for an extended journey or they are on their deathbed, they use their last few moments to say what is most important to them.

The last few chapters of Matthew describe Jesus's crucifixion and resurrection, a subject I'll discuss later. Matthew 28 records some of Jesus's last words on earth. Jesus is about to leave his disciples and return to heaven. The disciples obviously have mixed emotions about that. They are overjoyed that Jesus is alive, but now he is leaving again.

Knowing he will not see them again in this life, Jesus leaves them with several important thoughts. He isn't just speaking to them, of course—he is speaking to us. His last exhortations to his followers are as valid today as they were two thousand years ago.

Of all the things Jesus probably said that day, Matthew, the tax-collector-turned-disciple, chose to finish his book with these words: "And be sure of this: I am with you always, even to the end of the age." Clearly, this promise meant a lot to him.

With You Always

I'm sure Matthew was heartbroken at the thought of losing Jesus, especially after the emotional whiplash of seeing him crucified and then seeing him alive again. Jesus had indelibly altered the course of Matthew's life. Because Jesus had believed in him, because Jesus took time for him, Matthew had gone from being a notorious sinner to being one of Jesus's twelve disciples. Now Jesus was leaving physically, but he promised to always be there for them—to be here for us.

What does that mean? We can't see him. We can't hear him. We can't talk with him or hug him or laugh with him, at least not in a physical sense. When Jesus said he would be with his disciples, he wasn't talking about being physically present. That would be impossible, because even though he was God, he had taken on humanity and was limited to being in one place at a time.

Long before Jesus was crucified, he told his disciples that one day he would be killed, but he would return from the dead and then go back up to heaven. They refused to believe it. They even got on his case for being so negative. But he assured them it was actually better that way. He said God would send the Holy Spirit, who would be a comforter, counselor, and teacher.

The Holy Spirit is perhaps the least understood member of the Trinity, a term that describes how the Bible reveals God to us. The Bible teaches that God is one God who consists of three "persons": the Father, the Son (Jesus), and the Holy Spirit. Each person is distinct and fully God, yet there is only one God. That is why Jesus could be God while at the same time referring to his Father as God, and also promising that he would always be present with them through the Holy Spirit, who was God.

Confused? That's okay. God has it figured out. He's not having an identity crisis because we don't understand him completely. As humans, we are limited by our experience and frame of reference, so we have a tough time comprehending an infinite being. Actually, that's an understatement. It's not tough to fully comprehend God. It's impossible. If we could understand him, he wouldn't be God.

It's interesting how people try to redefine God to their liking. They bring him down to their level so they can understand him, then they reject him because he is too much like them.

A child has an easier time of it, because for a child, the world is full of wonder. I think as adults, we need a little more wonder in our lives. We need to relax a bit and allow ourselves to simply be in awe of God.

For some of us, right now, life has been blown a bit out of proportion. Maybe we are facing problems, or pain, or disease, or bankruptcy, and we know we need our perspective renewed by the magnitude and majesty of Jesus. We need to be in awe of God, not our problems.

Jesus is the resurrection and the life. Jesus is the victorious king of ages. Jesus rules and reigns, and he's sovereign, and he's big, and he's majestic, and he's strong, and he's able to help you with anything you are facing.

Jesus brought the presence of God to us permanently. As

I mentioned earlier, sin is no longer a barrier like it was in the days of Moses and the law. We don't have to beg God to come to us. We don't have to plead with him to pay attention to us. He is with us all the time.

Jesus is with you in your home, at your job, in your weaknesses and temptations and failures. Maybe you are facing the toughest situation you have ever faced in your life. Be assured, God is there. His voice calms the storm and gives you rest.

Jesus isn't just with you when you are doing well, or full of faith, or living in holiness. He loved you when you hated him, and he loves you now. He is head-over-heels in love with you. He is on your side not because of who you are but because of who he is. His love is unconditional and overwhelming. He is your advocate, your defense lawyer, and your biggest fan.

No problem is so big, no failure so permanent, and no enemy so powerful that Jesus can't give you the victory. Jesus speaks today, just as he did to his disciples so long ago.

"Be sure of this: I am with you always."

Why Are You Here?

Have you ever had somebody show up at your house unexpectedly? Maybe it's around dinnertime, and you're just getting ready to sit down and eat, and you hear the doorbell. You open it up, and it's a friend of yours.

And you're like, "Hey."

"Hey, I'm here."

"Great! Hi!" And you're frantically searching through your brain, trying to remember if you invited your friend over and just forgot or what. Finally you ask, "Uhh, why? Why are you here?"

"What do you mean? I'm just here."

"You're just here? Well, my family—we're sitting down for dinner, but—"

"Cool. Cool."

"Oh, so you came to eat?"

"No, I just came to be here."

It's just awkward.

We have to ask ourselves, why is Jesus with us?

This is where it goes to the next level, and a lot of people can't take it. They can agree that God is with them, but they just don't know why.

The Bible declares emphatically that God is with us *because God is for us*. He's here to make sure we're taken care of. He's here to hook us up and back us up. He's here to provide, protect, and empower.

Romans 8:31–32 makes this clear. "What shall we say about such wonderful things as these? If God is for us, who can ever be against us? Since he did not spare even his own Son but gave him up for us all, won't he also give us everything else?"

Some people argue this. That is unfathomable to me. Why would you argue that God is not for you?

Well, they say, sometimes he comes in his wrath, and he comes with judgment, and he comes—

Hold on. You mean to tell me that you don't think God is for you, even though he gave his Son for you? He's so for you that he died for you. What other proof do you need?

My dad used to ask people, "How good does God need to be to you before you're happy?" That's not a condemning statement. It's a wake-up call. We have a good God and we have a good Savior. Our lives are good. We have a lot to be grateful for and a lot to be happy about.

Some of us go so far as to think God gets a kick out of our suffering.

"Yeah, it's good for you to suffer. Grovel. Learn your lesson."

That's wrong. That's bizarre. If I were that kind of a parent, I would be put in jail for child abuse. Yet we attribute these strange, perverse motives to God.

I love what God says through the prophet Jeremiah: "'For I know the plans I have for you,' says the LORD. 'They are plans for good and not for disaster, to give you a future and a hope.'"

In other words, "Don't tell me I'm here to do you bad. Don't tell me I'm here to judge you. Don't tell me I'm here because I'm mad at you. I know the thoughts I think about you, and they're for good, not for evil. I know your future, and it is full of hope!"

God is with us, and he is for us. This is the gospel.

So no matter what I go through, he is with me and he is for me. Even if it doesn't make sense, he is with me and he is for me. Even if I can't cross every *t* and dot every *i*, he is with me and he is for me. No matter what anybody says, he is with me and he is for me. No matter what my emotions tell me, no matter what my bodily aches and pains tell me, no matter what my bank account tells me, he is with me and he is for me. He is on my side.

In the darkest part of your journey, the thing that will keep you full of life, peace, and happiness is the gospel. It's the knowledge that God is with you and for you.

Saved Alone

I suppose some could conclude that because Jesus is with us, everything will go well for us. Subtly, some of us might assume that the difference between those who love Jesus and those who don't is that the people who love him get all the desires of their hearts. So they'll have cars, and homes, and health, and strength. They will have abundant life because that's what Jesus promises.

Yes, God wants to bless you. Yes, God is for you. He's for your happiness, he's for your health, he's for your finances, and he's for your success.

But without a doubt, bad things happen to good people. Life is not always easy or pleasant. It doesn't always make sense. There are times we feel alone, abandoned, and hopeless.

When we understand that Jesus is here, however, we can make it through anything. People who know that Jesus loves them, who know that Jesus is with them and for them—those people can not only endure pain and loss and difficulty, they can come out the other side stronger and better people. They can be more alive than a person who sits in prosperous ease but is apart from Jesus.

Horatio Spafford was a prominent lawyer and business-man who lived in Chicago in the late 1800s. He was happily married and the proud father of four daughters and a four-year-old son. The Spafford family was well known in Chicago for their hospitality, their involvement in the abolitionist movement, and their support of Christian evangelists, including D. L. Moody. Horatio was heavily invested in Chicago real estate, the market was expanding, and life was good.

Then tragedy struck. In 1870, he lost his four-year-old son to scarlet fever. Just a few months later, the great Chicago fire hit, and his investments were destroyed.

Two years later, the family decided to vacation in Europe with some friends. The date came for them to go on the ship, but at the last moment, Horatio was detained by real-estate business. So he sent his wife and four daughters ahead on the ship S.S. *Ville de Havre*, intending to go over later.

After several days, he received a now-famous cable from his wife. It began, "Saved alone. What shall I do . . ."

He soon learned the terrible news: the ship bearing his family had collided with another ship in the open sea. Within twelve minutes, the *Ville de Havre* had gone under. All four daughters drowned. The only thing he knew to do now was to get on the next ship over so he could console his wife.

The ship set sail. Horatio had time to reflect on the horrific two years he had lived. Some distance into the journey, the captain notified Horatio that they had reached the spot where the *Ville de Havre* had gone down just a few weeks prior. This was the watery grave of his beloved daughters.

It was in that moment, at that spot in the open sea, that Horatio Spafford began to write a poem of sorts. He penned words to describe where he was emotionally and spiritually.

What he wrote has become one of the most-loved hymns of all time:

> *When peace like a river attendeth my way,*
> *When sorrows like sea billows roll:*
> *Whatever my lot, Thou has taught me to say,*
> *It is well, it with well with my soul.*

As a father, I cannot imagine enduring such loss. The financial disaster was tough enough. But to lose a baby boy, then two years later to lose four daughters?

And now, in the loneliness and vastness of the open sea, instead of shaking his fist at God and complaining, Horatio revealed that he was still very much aware of Jesus. Even in the midst of his pain, his loss, and his hurt, he knew Jesus was with him.

The Bible says, "Though I walk through the valley of the shadow of death, I will fear no evil; for You are with me" (Psalm 23:4 NKJV).

When we have Jesus, we have everything we will ever need for anything we could ever go through. Maybe things aren't going smoothly for us right now. Maybe everything isn't wonderful. Maybe we are in the open sea of hurt and pain and loss.

Jesus gives us the grace to stand and say, "It is well with my soul," because he is here. In the midst of loss and death, our souls can find rest and life.

Jesus Wept

I am not minimizing loss. I am not implying that we should suppress our grief or criticize those who mourn. Far from it. The death of my father was a journey of sorrow and grief that rocked me to my core. I spent months processing my feelings and trying to regain my sense of identity after my father was gone.

But through the rollercoaster years of sickness, through my father's passing, and through suddenly finding myself responsible for leading a church of thousands of people, I was never alone.

Jesus was alive, and Jesus was with me. He was my life, my peace, my assurance. I don't claim to have had a perfect attitude; Horatio Spafford is my hero. But I found a depth of love and strength in Jesus that I had never known before. I experienced the simplicity of the gospel and the power of grace.

I wish I could put into words the presence of Jesus that strengthened me, but maybe it's something that must be experienced to be understood. What I can tell you is that it is there when we need it. Jesus is more real, more present, more alive, and more united with us than we know. Sometimes it takes tragic circumstances to realize how real our faith is.

"Here on earth you will have many trials and sorrows," Jesus said. "But take heart, because I have overcome the world" (John 16:33).

The story of Lazarus's death that we discussed earlier shows Jesus's love and empathy when we go through difficult experiences. John 11:35, one of the shortest but most profound verses in the Bible, says, "Then Jesus wept." Jesus doesn't scorn our grief. He weeps with us.

If you read the rest of that story, you figure out Jesus knew the whole time that Lazarus would die, and Jesus knew he was going to raise him from the dead. So why weep? Why waste his tears? Why not instead rebuke the people for their lack of faith, or take the opportunity to point out his own power and divinity?

He wept because their grief moved him. Their sorrow aroused his compassion.

But Jesus didn't just grieve with them. He raised Lazarus

from the dead, and he brings life to us as well. The life of Jesus is most clearly revealed in moments of apparent death.

"I am the resurrection and the life," Jesus told Martha. "Anyone who believes in me will live, even after dying. Everyone who lives in me and believes in me will never ever die" (John 11:25–26).

The fact that Jesus is here not only brings comfort in hard times, it gives us courage that our circumstances can change. Jesus brings life out of death. He brings hope out of sorrow. He turns our mourning into joy. Jesus is there for us when we need him most—whether we know it or not and whether we appreciate it or not.

Jesus will never leave us. He will never abandon us. He will never give up on us.

Jesus is always here.

JESUS IS alive.

THIRTEEN

Real Life

I enjoy movies. That may be a shock to you because I'm a pastor, and you probably thought pastors only watch TBN and VeggieTales.

Lest you think me unspiritual, I will neither confirm nor deny whether I have actually seen the movie that I'm about to quote from. Let's just say I've heard from other people who saw it. They told me it's violent, and I'm not for violence. So like I said, I can neither confirm nor deny that I've seen this movie.

The movie is *Braveheart*. I've been told that in this movie, William Wallace makes a certain profound statement. So, of course, I did some research. I used some of my incredible resources, such as Wikipedia, and I discovered that we're not sure if William Wallace said this particular quote. But we certainly know Mel Gibson did.

"Every man dies, but not every man truly lives."

What a concept. It's worth thinking about.

That's the Life

Are you alive? You are breathing, you are functioning, your brain is more or less engaged, and you are reading this book. So yes, you are alive. You even have official documents that prove your existence to anyone who might question it. You are sucking oxygen on planet Earth. You are alive.

But are you *really* living?

The apostle Paul described what it means to be truly alive in Ephesians 2:1–7.

> And you He made alive, who were dead in trespasses and sins, in which you once walked according to the course of this world, according to the prince of the power of the air, the spirit who now works in the sons of disobedience, among whom also we all once conducted ourselves in the lusts of our flesh, fulfilling the desires of the flesh and of the mind, and were by nature children of wrath, just as the others.
>
> But God, who is rich in mercy, because of His great love with which He loved us, even when we were dead in trespasses, made us alive together with Christ (by grace you have been saved), and raised us up together, and made us sit together in the heavenly places in Christ Jesus, that in the ages to come He might show the exceeding riches of His grace in His kindness toward us in Christ Jesus. (NKJV)

Many of us are always in hot pursuit of "the life." For example, we're stuck in traffic on a bridge, and we look down and see people waterskiing below and say, "Man, that's the life. I need to get myself a boat. That would really be living."

Or we watch our boss come in late and leave early every day, and we've been in his corner office with the big windows and we know all he does is play Angry Birds. It's not fair, because we work forty, fifty, sixty hours a week and barely scrape by. And we think, *My boss is really living the life. I want his job. Then I could finally enjoy life.*

But would living "the life" really satisfy us? To truly live, do we just need more money? A promotion? A boat?

Those things are nice. Especially the boat. But in the pursuit of true life, they are red herrings. Just decoys. That's why many people go their whole lives without ever truly living. That's what Solomon discovered, as we saw earlier in Ecclesiastes.

Oh, sure, we all have our moments. This life will offer us good moments and laughter and joy and exhilaration and fun. But the truth is, at the end of the day, we lay our heads on our pillows at night and we know something's not right.

A marriage can't make you truly alive. A second marriage can't make you truly alive. A bank account can't make you truly alive. Popularity can't make you truly alive. And your new twenty-four-inch rims can't make you truly alive. They may look good, but they can't bring life.

Missing the Mark

Let me go a step further. Is living in sin really living?

I suppose before we answer that question, we need to establish the reality of sin. If you have a toddler, you already know sin is real. And it wears diapers. How can something so cute get so mad and so loud? In the mall? When everyone is watching? No one has to teach us to be selfish, ungrateful, and angry. That's the factory default. We are born with a bent toward sin, which the Bible calls a sinful nature.

Lots of sincere people have tried to explain away sin, but the fact remains, there are evil people out there. All it takes is for someone to hit your mama and you know there is sin in the world. Even "good" people do a lot of evil things. Sin is all over the place. It's in me and it's in you.

God created Adam and Eve, the first man and the first woman, with a free will because he did not want a relationship with a bunch of Pinocchios. He wanted us to be able to pull our own strings, to make our own choices. He knew that forced love is not love at all. So God gave us the ability within ourselves to choose him or reject him. Adam and Eve rejected God, and now throughout the ages, humans are born with a tendency to reject God and go their own way. That departure from God's original plan is the root of all sin.

So right and wrong exist. I'm not one of those people who believe that what's all right for you is all right for you, and what's all right for me is all right for me. That breaks down pretty quickly when what's right for me hurts you. Suddenly you don't think it's right anymore. There are absolutes out there. Good people strive to abide by them, and good governments enforce them.

Then there are areas that are amoral—neither right nor wrong. Most of life is that way, actually. As long as we handle them properly, these areas can contribute to our joy and success. Money, for example, is amoral. Cars are amoral. Sports are amoral, except for maybe cricket—any game that takes five days to play must be sin. Apologies to my British friends.

There are also things that are wrong in certain contexts. In that sense, morality can be relative. In Singapore, for instance, it's basically a crime to chew gum. But here in Seattle, we have a city landmark called the Gum Wall. It's down by Pike's Market, and people from all over the world, including probably Singapore, come and stick their nasty gum wad to a wall in an alley. It the most disgusting thing you could imagine. But it's not sin. I wish it were, but it's not.

The best definition I've heard for sin is *missing the mark.* There is a mark. God established it. And we have all missed it.

There is nothing relative or contextual or gray about it. Sin is sin. Wrong is wrong. No matter how we spin it, no matter what we call it, we have all sinned, and we continue to sin more often than we'd like to admit.

The first mention of sin in the Bible is in Genesis 4:7. Cain is angry with his brother Abel, and God warns him not to give in to sin. "If you refuse to do what is right, then watch out! Sin is crouching at the door, eager to control you. But you must subdue it and be its master."

If you've heard the story, you know that Cain didn't subdue sin. Not even close. He went out and killed his brother. It was the first murder in human history.

Ruling over sin is a nice sentiment, but the human race has never been very good at it. The Bible tells us time and time again that we are all sinners. Romans 3:23 says plainly, "For everyone has sinned; we all fall short of God's glorious standard."

Romans 3:10 says the same thing: "No one is righteous— not even one." To be righteous means you're in right standing with God. To be righteous means you can stand shoulder to shoulder with God because you are right and you are sinless and you are perfect. The Bible says there is not even one person like that.

We can try to be righteous. And I suppose we all do. We help an elderly lady cross the street, we open the door for somebody, we give five bucks to a homeless guy on the street corner. We do good things to try to fill the void inside that keeps telling us something's wrong. But in all our do-goodism, in all the hours we put in at work, in all our efforts to better our marriages and be good fathers or good mothers or good uncles or good aunts, something is still wrong.

The passage I quoted out of Ephesians says that we were dead in our sins. In other words, life under sin is not life at all. It's death. No matter how many boats we own, if we are ruled by sin, we aren't alive. We're all card-carrying members of the walking dead. We have our moments, we do our best, but we're still not experiencing true life.

Can life in sin be called living? Not really. Sure, we're breathing. Sin will let us breathe for a while—but it will never let us truly live. That's how sin works.

So I've got good news and bad news. The bad news is, we are all sinners. The good news is, if you are a sinner, you fit right in with the rest of us.

Don't Vote for Pedro

So where do we go? What do we do? Can we find a man or a woman we can nominate and vote into office who can solve the sin problem? Can we pass some powerful, profound legislation that will set humanity free from the sin problem? Is that our answer?

The problem with nominating one of our own is, that person

also has a sin problem. We can wink and look away and pretend everything is good, but the Bible clearly says we have all sinned. So the answer is not among us. The answer is not in one of our own. A Republican can't help us. A Democrat can't help us. Pedro definitely can't help us. No offense, Napoleon Dynamite.

The apostle Paul wrote Ephesians. Before he got to know God, Paul was not a good man. He thought he was a good man because he was a religious fanatic. But he barged into people's homes and dragged them off to jail because they didn't believe what he did. He was mean. He was arrogant. He was an accomplice to murder.

Then God got a hold of his life, and everything changed. He ended up writing nearly half the books of the New Testament.

Yet even after becoming one of the greatest spiritual leaders in the history of the church, he still lost the battle against sin from time to time. In Romans 7:24, he voices the cry of all humanity: "Oh, what a miserable person I am! Who will free me from this life that is dominated by sin and death?"

Paul was expressing the tenacious, ubiquitous nature of sin. He knew that sin sneaks up on us, that sin tries to control us. In the next verse, Paul answers his own question: "Thank God! The answer is in Jesus Christ our Lord."

Jesus is the only man who has ever truly lived, because sin had no hold on him. It's sin that sucks the life out of our existence.

Jesus showed up on the planet brimming with life because he knew no sin. Sure, he was tempted; but he resisted all temptation, and he lived for thirty-three years without sin.

Because he was the only person who ever truly lived, he is the only one who could solve the sin problem once and for all.

He made a way for us to get back to really living.

JESUS IS _____.

Keep Swinging

The first few verses of Ephesians 2 paint a very bleak picture of what life looks like apart from God and apart from Jesus. But then we get to verse four.

"But God . . ."

I love it when God butts in.

And by the way, when God butted in right here, it wasn't because we e-mailed him. It wasn't because we called him. It wasn't because we sent someone out waving a white flag to tell God, "We're really sorry. We apologize for ignoring you. We'd like you to get involved with humanity again."

In fact, we ignored him as much as we always did. We were enjoying missing the mark. We were getting grins and giggles out of our sins and transgressions.

"But God"—while we were still sinners, Christ died for us.

"But God"—he took the initiative.

"But God"—he was driven by his own rich mercy and great love.

That's good stuff right there. God is "rich in mercy." He doesn't just have mercy—he has mercy with all kinds of layers. Mercy that knows no end. Mercy in abundance. The Bible says that mercy triumphs over judgment. What we deserved for our wrongdoing, for rejecting the Creator, was judgment. But God is rich in mercy. God is a God of second chances.

I know about second chances because my two boys played T-ball. Are you serious? The ball is stationary on a rubber T. How many swings do these kids get? It's the eighth swing, and parents in the stands are saying, "Good swing, Johnny!"

174

I'm thinking, "He didn't even hit the rubber T and it's three feet in front of him. Why are we celebrating this mediocrity?"

Then on the eighth swing, he brushes the bottom of the T, and the ball falls off. And the coach yells, "Run!"

That's a lot like God. We get one strike, then another strike, then another—and everybody is saying, "I can't believe this guy is still alive. I can't believe God is still blessing him."

We keep swinging and swinging. And God, who is rich in mercy, picks up the ball again. "Swing again, slugger. Just swing again."

Meanwhile, people watching us are shaking their heads. "He's out."

God says, "He's not out till I say he's out."

Ephesians 2 says that not only is God rich in mercy, he also has "great love." I like that phrase. Not just love—it's great love. I love a few people in this world, but my love is far from great. It's limited, and it falters, and it often has a selfish tinge to it.

But God loves the world.

Who is this God with such layers of mercy and such amazing, great love? Who is this God who seeks out people who are dead and brings them to life not because of their merit or their potential but because he is full of mercy and love?

Some of us think God loves us because we have potential. *We look bad now,* we think, *but God saves us because we will amount to something someday.*

"Hey Gabriel," we imagine God saying to his head angel. "Do you see that guy over there?"

"Uh, that walking disaster?"

"Yeah, that's the one. He's got potential."

"What? No way, God. You're wasting your time."

"No really—I can see it," we imagine God saying. "Once I work him over for a few years, he's going to be a productive Christian. I think he can help me out."

That sounds spiritual. That sounds humble. But it's not. It's actually just another way of saying we deserved to be saved. Maybe we didn't do anything yet, but we flatter ourselves into thinking that God saved us because he knew what we could become.

Listen, God doesn't save us because we have potential. That's ridiculous. We do have potential—that much is true—but God doesn't rescue us from the death of sin just so we can help him out. He doesn't need our help.

He just wants to love us. He wants to be loved by us.

That would be like saying I had kids just so I would have someone to clean my house. Please. Anyone who has kids is laughing at the idea. When you have kids around, even the bar of soap is dirty. But that's okay. We don't mind, at least most of the time. Kids are absolutely the most fulfilling thing in life outside of God and marriage.

My wife and I chose to have kids because we longed for a family relationship. In a very real sense, we loved them before they even existed. It had nothing to do with their potential to clean house or pay bills. It was our initiative, motivated by our love.

God saw us, dead in our sins, and he couldn't sit still. His rich mercy and his great love propelled him to provide a way to bring us back to life.

That's why he sent Jesus.

In Jesus, every person can truly live.

FOURTEEN

Zombie Jesus

The Gospel of Matthew ends on a spectacular note. Earlier, I quoted the final verse, in which Jesus promises to be with us always. Actually, the entire final chapter is an exclamation mark celebrating the greatest victory in Jesus's life and challenging us with a glorious future.

The setting is right after Jesus's death. The Roman government was relieved because the guy who had sparked so much civil unrest was no longer their problem. The Pharisees were ecstatic, because their competition had been eliminated. The disciples were terrified and confused because this was not at all how they visualized things working out.

Here is chapter 28:

Early on Sunday morning, as the new day was dawning, Mary Magdalene and the other Mary went out to visit the tomb.

Suddenly there was a great earthquake! For an angel of the Lord came down from heaven, rolled aside the stone, and sat on it. His face shone like lightning, and his clothing was as white as snow. The guards shook with fear when they saw him, and they fell into a dead faint.

Then the angel spoke to the women. "Don't be afraid!" he said. "I know you are looking for Jesus, who was crucified. He isn't here! He is risen from the dead, just as he said would happen. Come, see where his body was lying. And now, go quickly and tell his disciples that he has risen from the dead, and he is going ahead of you to Galilee. You will see him there. Remember what I have told you."

The women ran quickly from the tomb. They were very frightened but also filled with great joy, and they rushed to give the disciples the angel's message. And as they went, Jesus met them and greeted them. And they ran to him, grasped his feet, and worshiped him. Then Jesus said to them, "Don't be afraid! Go tell my brothers to leave for Galilee, and they will see me there."

As the women were on their way, some of the guards went into the city and told the leading priests what had happened. A meeting with the elders was called, and they decided to give the soldiers a large bribe. They told the soldiers, "You must say, 'Jesus's disciples came during the night while we were sleeping, and they stole his body.' If the governor hears about it, we'll stand up for you so you won't get in trouble." So the guards accepted the bribe and said what they were told to say. Their story spread widely among the Jews, and they still tell it today.

Then the eleven disciples left for Galilee, going to the mountain where Jesus had told them to go. When they saw him, they worshiped him—but some of them doubted!

Jesus came and told his disciples, "I have been given all authority in heaven and on earth. Therefore, go and make disciples of all the nations, baptizing them in the name of the Father and the Son and the Holy Spirit. Teach these new disciples to obey all the commands I have given you. And be sure of this: I am with you always, even to the end of the age."

I'm Back

In one moment, everything changed. This was the ultimate happy ending, the original buzzer-beater. Everyone knew Jesus was dead. They saw the Roman soldiers execute him, and Roman soldiers were professionals at killing people.

But now, he's alive. He's popping up in random places, scaring the heck out of his already jittery disciples, and saying, "I'm back." For some reason I always imagine an Austrian accent.

The Romans and the Pharisees are left scrambling, while the disciples are out of their minds with joy. A few of Jesus's followers needed some convincing because like many of us, they were more prone to believe bad news than good news.

Really? Jesus must have thought. *I come back from the dead and my friends don't even recognize me. Lame.*

But Jesus was back, just as he had promised.

And speaking of zombie apocalypses—which we weren't, but my brain works like that—you could call Jesus the ultimate zombie. He was killed, then he came back from the dead, and now he's coming for you.

Okay—some of you would do well to discover a sense of humor. You'll live longer.

Here's the deal. If Jesus just died and that was it, there's nothing remarkable about that. People die all the time—even good people. It's part of being human.

Lots of people have even given their lives for their beliefs. We remember them as martyrs, and their legacy inspires us, and sometimes we get a day off work in their honor, but that is about it.

But if it's true Jesus rose from the dead, then that changes everything. That means he conquered the final enemy: death. That means everything he claimed about himself is true. He isn't just human. He is God. He is the answer to mankind's problems. He is the Savior.

The Pharisees figured this out quicker than many of us. Whether they actually thought he came back to life or not, we don't know. I suspect some of them did, but they couldn't process it. They couldn't adjust their thinking. They didn't want a bigger perspective. They didn't want to mess with the status quo.

They knew what would happen if rumor got out that he was back. It would undermine their entire way of life. The religious authorities would no longer be the way to God; Jesus would be the way to God. Sinners would no longer be excluded from salvation; they would be prime candidates for salvation. People would no longer strive to follow impossible laws; they would follow Jesus, whose yoke was easy and whose burden was light, and they would live in the wide open spaces of grace.

So they lied. And they bribed the Roman guards to spread the lie. And they promised to protect the guards whom they had bribed. Yes, it was messy, but it was better than accepting that the laws of the universe had been upended because God himself, the maker of the laws, had been in their midst but they didn't recognize him.

I don't mean to criticize sincere people, but a lot of good people go to great lengths to avoid the conclusion that Jesus is God. They can accept that he was a good man—even a great man. They lament the fact that such a nice guy died for what he believed. "It's sad. People are so awful to each other sometimes." They wish he could have continued his career as an enlightened spiritual teacher. They hold up his teachings on love and justice as an ideal for humanity to pursue. And they feel bad, and they put on a long face, and they go back to their lives and their problems with the same limited perspective as everyone around them.

But Jesus didn't just die. He rose from the dead.

That's what a God would do, because an eternal, infinite God can't be killed—at least not permanently—by his creation. The resurrection proves that everything he said was true. It gives us all hope that we can live in victory in this life. It proves that life continues after our time on earth is over.

The gospel is good news because of the resurrection. The gospel isn't just that Jesus died for our sins. That's the first half. The second half is that Jesus rose again, proving once and for all that sin and death were conquered and we can have eternal life.

Hollow Chocolate Bunnies

When I was growing up, my parents bought me a chocolate Easter bunny every year. And every year, I would open the box, pull out the bunny, and bite off an ear, hoping that this would be the year that the bunny was actually solid chocolate. It never was. It was hollow. Every stinking year. Why was I never allowed the luxury of having a solid chocolate Easter bunny? Why?

Paul wrote in 1 Corinthians 15:16–20,

> And if there is no resurrection of the dead, then Christ has not been raised. And if Christ has not been raised, then your faith is useless and you are still guilty of your sins. In that case, all who have died believing in Christ are lost! And if our hope in Christ is only for this life, we are more to be pitied than anyone in the world. But in fact, Christ has been raised from the dead. He is the first of a great harvest of all who have died.

Paul is telling the Christians in Corinth that if Jesus was not raised from the dead, then their faith was as hollow as a chocolate Easter bunny. No substance. No meaning. No point. Just a sham.

If Jesus didn't rise again, it means we are still in our sins. His death didn't work. It wasn't good enough. He wasn't strong enough to defeat the final enemy, death.

We have to understand that death was not part of God's original creation. It was an effect of sin. So if death defeated Jesus, then sin has not been dealt with, and we are still lost in our sin.

He goes so far as to say that if Christianity is about being good little boys and girls in this life and nothing more, then we are the most pitiful creatures on the planet.

In other words, this life is not the point. This life is wonderful, and God has good things for us while we are here on earth. But Jesus didn't give his life to promote a moral code of conduct. He didn't suffer and die for world peace. Our faith isn't about studying the Bible, or praying, or going to church. All of those things are good, but Jesus's victory was bigger.

Jesus came so we could live forever with him. That's true life.

No Matter What, We Win

The Bible talks a lot about miracles and divine healing. In our church, we have prayed for many sick people and have seen genuine healings, even in very difficult situations. Not everyone has been healed, but many have. I am convinced of God's willingness and his power to heal the sick, just as Jesus did so many years ago.

So when my father received that terrible diagnosis of cancer, my family and our church fought the good fight of faith. We prayed continually for my dad. We stood on the promises of the Bible and believed that God would heal his body and prolong his life.

The people in our church are amazing, let me just say that. Their outpouring of love in that season still moves me to tears. My family will forever be in their debt. We walked through the valley of the shadow of death together, and even in the darkest of times, they did not waver in their faith.

For several years my dad had almost no symptoms of cancer. The treatments had difficult side effects at times, but the cancer itself seemed to be controlled. Our faith was high. Our prayers were energetic and full of confidence.

After several more years, however, he began to worsen significantly. His blood counts deteriorated. Pain increased. The treatments were slowing the progress of the cancer, but his health had taken a definite turn for the worse.

As circumstances changed, we were all forced to question what we really believed about God, about death, and about the meaning of life. I don't think we doubted God's goodness or power to heal, but we had to wrestle with questions we never thought we would face.

What if Pastor Wendell doesn't get healed? You could tell it was on everyone's mind. *For years now, we've been praying for his healing, believing for his healing, talking about how sure we are that he is going to be healed—but what if he dies? What happens to our faith then?*

I had recently become the preaching pastor of our church. My dad was still the senior pastor, but because of his health he was rarely able to preach. So every weekend, I would stand before the church and declare the goodness and power of God. And every weekend, I could see the questions in people's eyes.

But my parents' faith was unquenchable, and all of us took heart and grew in faith as we watched them. My dad said it best: "No matter what happens, we win."

That was what I affirmed to people week after week from the pulpit. Whether God healed him or took him home, we could not lose. If he were healed, that would be a tremendous victory. But if not, heaven would not be a concession. Heaven would not be defeat.

In 2010, a few days before Christmas, my dad passed away. He is in a better place—an infinitely better place. He finished his race, he fought the good fight of faith, and he passed the baton to the next generation. Now, I believe he's looking down on me and on our church, cheering us on.

We were sad, of course, and the loss was difficult. We still miss him every single day. But our perspective in this life is based on eternity. We know we will see him again. We know that God's goodness and love and power are as real as ever.

The Bible calls death the final enemy. It's a bigger enemy than sickness, doubt, fear, sin, poverty, or pain. Jesus conquered this final enemy in the resurrection. That means we don't have to fear anything—even death. I firmly believe that heaven was the ultimate victory for my dad. Death did not defeat him, because Jesus had already defeated death.

Romans 5:21 says, "So just as sin ruled over all people and brought them to death, now God's wonderful grace rules instead, giving us right standing with God and resulting in eternal life through Jesus Christ our Lord." Sin, death, and the devil hold no threat when we know who we are in Jesus.

This is how we gain perspective in life. It's the gospel that brings things back into proportion. Bad news abounds, but the good news of the gospel trumps it every time. Obstacles may loom large, but Jesus is greater than them all.

The Sky Is (Not) Falling

Sometimes Christians are the biggest doomsayers of all. It's not healthy. Frankly, it's not even Christian. Fearfulness is an indictment against our God.

Some of us go into a state of complete consternation when the person we voted for doesn't get elected, or when we hear of wars or disasters. We think it's the end of the world. It's Armageddon.

Sorry, but I don't subscribe to the notion that the world is a hopeless mess and we just have to hang on till Jesus comes back. I refuse to stockpile guns and gold, build a tree house in Montana, and wait for the world to go up in smoke.

Our tendency to overreact to bad news is, unfortunately, legendary. We can only cry "It's the end of the world!" so many times before people lump us in with Chicken Little and the boy who cried wolf.

It's bizarre, but some people actually enjoy bad news, even people who claim to believe that God is in control. They are fearmongers. They deal in worst-case scenarios. They traffic terror and peddle panic.

News flash—regardless of the state of the world or the poll results of your favorite politician, Jesus is still in control. He wasn't voted in and he can't be voted out. He rules and reigns over the affairs of mankind.

Because Jesus lives, I can live differently. I can act and react from a place of peace and an attitude of assurance.

Jesus is in control of my past, my present, and my future. Despair over my past failures or fear over future problems cannot control my present because Jesus rules me with peace.

God says in a poetic passage in Isaiah: "Heaven is my throne, and the earth is my footstool" (66:1). In other words, God is far bigger than we are. His perspective of the planet is not limited to time and space.

In another passage in Isaiah, he says, "My thoughts are nothing like your thoughts . . . and my ways are far beyond anything you could imagine. For just as the heavens are higher than the earth, so my ways are higher than your ways and my thoughts higher than your thoughts" (55:8–10).

I'm convinced that in comparison to God, we cannot make our problems small enough. We cannot make Satan small enough. We cannot make sin and sickness small enough. When we consider the magnitude and majesty of our all-powerful, all-knowing God, when we realize Jesus is here with us no matter what turns or twists our lives take, we find peace.

Some people think Jesus and Satan are about equal in power. They think good and evil are duking it out in some cosmic boxing ring, and the fate of the universe depends on this match. It's the fifteenth round, and we're in the stands, hoping against hope that Jesus pulls off a victory, but it doesn't look good. Evil seems to be winning.

Every time Jesus takes it on the chin, we grimace and we groan. Someone yells out, "My God, somebody call the fight. He's bleeding! He's taking too many punches!"

Jesus goes to his corner with his trainer, the Holy Spirit. And the Holy Spirit is telling him, "Just keep dancing. Keep juking and diving. Maybe there's still a chance."

People in the stands are thinking, *Man, I hope Jesus makes a comeback.*

Wait—what? A comeback? Where do we come up with this stuff? Jesus is God. God does not make comebacks. When you're God and nobody else is God, you're never behind.

My dad used to say, "We serve a great big God and we are opposed by a little bitty devil." Let's not get that backward. There is no doubt who will be the winner in the struggle between good and evil because Jesus's death and resurrection already dealt Satan a fatal blow. The devil is nothing but a dog on a leash. He is a toothless lion. He is a magician hiding behind a curtain, trying to manipulate us through smoke and mirrors. Just read the end of the Bible. We win.

I'm not worried about the state of the union, the state of the universe, or the state of my finances. I'm going to go to sleep tonight with a smile on my face not just because I get to sleep next to the most beautiful woman in the world but because Jesus is in control.

That's not irresponsibility, gullibility, or naiveté. It's true life.

FIFTEEN

New Way to Be Human

I want to prepare you for what I am about to say. I don't want you to think less of me, but I'm going to be really honest and transparent here.

When Michael Jackson passed away a couple of years ago, I listened to all his songs. Multiple times. And I enjoyed them.

All right? There it is. I just got it off my chest.

I'm not saying all his songs have the most godly lyrics. That's why some of you are like, "Michael who?"

Yeah, don't give me that religious look. I know you have the *Free Willy* song on your iPod.

Actually, one of his songs illustrates what I want to say in this chapter. It's called "Human Nature," and it's from the album *Thriller*, which I know you know nothing about, because you have been reading your Bible and listening to Pavarotti. But this album did pretty well, even if you've never heard of it.

Sometimes I feel for my wife, because I'll get songs stuck in my mind and I sing them over and over. Only it's a challenge for me to remember the actual words of a song, so I either say the same thing again and again or I make stuff up. It's a real test of my wife's faith.

The chorus goes, "If they say 'why, why?' Tell 'em that it's human nature."

It's a catchy line, but of course that's all I can remember of the song. So for a couple of days, I walked around the house singing, "Why, why? Tell 'em that it's human nature ..."

And my wife is going, "Oh my gosh, Judah. Please."

At the time, I had been spending a lot of time thinking about a passage in Colossians. And I realized that actually, this song by the King of Pop illustrates the premise of that passage pretty well. Colossians 3:1–11 says,

> Since you have been raised to new life with Christ, set your sights on the realities of heaven, where Christ sits in the place of honor at God's right hand. Think about the things of heaven, not the things of earth. For you died to this life, and your real life is hidden with Christ in God. And when Christ, who is your life, is revealed to the whole world, you will share in all his glory.
>
> So put to death the sinful, earthly things lurking within you. Have nothing to do with sexual immorality, impurity, lust, and evil desires. Don't be greedy, for a greedy person is an idolater, worshiping the things of this world. Because of these sins, the anger of God is coming. You used to do these things when your life was still part of this world. But now is the time to get rid of anger, rage, malicious behavior, slander, and dirty language. Don't lie to each other, for you have stripped off your old sinful nature and all its wicked deeds. Put on your new

nature, and be renewed as you learn to know your Creator and become like him. In this new life, it doesn't matter if you are a Jew or a Gentile, circumcised or uncircumcised, barbaric, uncivilized, slave, or free. Christ is all that matters, and he lives in all of us.

All of us can relate to Michael Jackson's song because, unfortunately, we are all incredibly familiar with human nature. It's a part of who we are.

But here's the big idea of this passage. It's actually the subtitle of this whole book. That's how important this understanding is.

Jesus gives us a new way to be human.

In Jesus, and only in Jesus, we are offered a new way of living. When Jesus rose from the dead, we rose from the dead, too, on a spiritual level. Someday we'll physically rise, too, but for now we have a new spiritual life, a new nature.

We can actually transcend human nature. We don't have to be subject to all our impulses and urges, to all of our desires and passions.

Now I am not just a "normal" human. I have a new way of living. I am a new kind of human. Because of Jesus, we have a new humanity.

Jesus on Monday

A lot of us go to church on Sunday and listen to a preacher talk about Jesus. We hear how Jesus helps us transcend our humanity and live in holiness. We hear that Jesus gives us grace.

Then we wake up Monday morning, and something happens. We go from the motto, "I am who I am by the grace of God" to "God helps those who help themselves."

FYI, only the first motto is backed up by the Bible.

So we think, *Well, Jesus was great for Sunday, but now Monday's here, so I gotta get my work on. If I'm going to get anything, it's because I'm going to work at it. And God is going to bless me because he blesses those who work really hard.*

So we work our backsides off all week, and we get all beat down and frustrated, then we go back to church the following Sunday, and we say, "Wow, this is a good message on Jesus."

Sounds a bit schizophrenic, right? And we are wearing ourselves out because we think Jesus is for Sunday and work is for the rest of the week. I don't want to just talk about Jesus, sing about Jesus, and preach about Jesus on Sunday. I want Jesus every day, in every area of my life.

Sit Down

In Colossians 3, Paul outlines for us what it looks like to live grace Monday through Saturday. Notice his opening words: "If then . . ." It's a simple phrase that has massive implications. It means, "Based on everything I'm saying, do this."

If you read back, you'll find Paul has just taken two chapters to extol the incredible grace of God at work in our lives. He has laid a groundwork based on Jesus and his work on the cross. He described how Jesus is at the center of everything. He says that our old, sinful nature died and was buried with him. When Jesus was resurrected, we were also raised to life, spiritually speaking, but now we have a new nature—a divine nature.

Then he starts chapter 3 by saying, "Hey, taking into account everything I'm saying about Jesus, about grace, and about your new nature, here is what you need to do."

I'm glad that Colossians 3 isn't Colossians 1. If Paul had started the letter to the Colossians by reciting a list of dos and don'ts—without laying the theological foundation of Jesus at the center—we would still be living by the law, depending on our deeds to open the door to God.

I love how Paul puts the ball in our court: "So, have you been raised with Christ or not? Yes or no?"

"Well, yes."

"Are you sure? You don't sound sure."

"Yes, I'm sure. I have been raised."

"OK, you've been raised with Christ. Based on that fact, then, seek those things which are above."

In other words, make sure you don't base your obedience on anything other than the finished work of Jesus. Don't keep straining and striving to be righteous based on your own merit like you used to. You have a new nature now.

The passage I quoted above uses an odd word to describe Jesus. It says he *sits* in heaven. Sits? He is seated? Lounging with his feet kicked up and a cold drink in his hand? Shouldn't he be pacing the sidelines, yelling at his team to run the play, make the pass, beat the opposition?

Standing implies action. Urgency. Activity. Jesus should be standing.

But Jesus is sitting.

Sitting is the position of reigning. Jesus is not on his feet.

He is not walking around, stalking around, pacing around. He is not biting his nails. He is not sweating.

Jesus is sitting. He is relaxing and he is chillaxing. He is in heaven, and all is well. All is finished. He sits there at the right hand of God, the Bible says, and he laughs at his enemies, and he makes the entire earth his ottoman.

If we would orient our lives around the reality that Jesus is sitting in heaven, it would affect our Mondays.

The first position of a believer is not walking. It's not pacing. It's not marching. It's not sprinting madly from one activity to the next.

It's sitting. When we were born again, we were called to rest in his finished work.

God is telling us, "Just sit down."

And we're like, "No, God, I got this."

"Sit down."

"But, I've got to do—I've got to go—"

"Sit down."

When you wake up in the morning, or when you are working hard to support your family and pay your bills, or when you start to stress about your future—remember to sit down. Remember to orient your life around the reality of Jesus. Remember, it is not by your strength, your power, your ingenuity, or your education. It is the work of Jesus.

It's Who I Am

The devil would love for us to believe that sin is not completely defeated, that somehow our particular sin slipped through the cross, and even Jesus could not kill it off. So now, we're stuck with it. It owns us. It defines us. It's our pet sin, our inner demon, our personal vice.

The devil is a liar. Sin is defeated. God is for us, Jesus is with us, and his grace is sufficient.

At some point in our lives, we will sin again. And chances are, it's not too far off. But Jesus knew that, and he saved us anyway. In one moment of grace and faith, he forgave every sin you have committed, are committing, and will commit.

Here is a thought that blows my mind: God sees character flaws in me that I don't even see, and he is not stressed about it. He is not planning to work on some of those areas for another thirty years. I'll be sixty-three years old, and one morning God will say to me, "Judah, here's an area we are going to start working on now." And in the meantime, he's not frustrated with me. He's not stiff-arming me when I try to draw close. He's not quarantining me lest I infect someone else. He is telling me that he is proud of me, that he is pleased with me, that I am amazing.

We get in such a hurry to perfect ourselves, because we think that as soon as we do, God will love us more.

But he will never love us more than he does right now. He will never accept us more than he does right now.

God is not in a hurry to fix us. Our behavior is not his first priority. We are his first priority. Loving us, knowing us, affirming us, protecting us. That is his top goal and his main concern.

Our fight against sin is noble and good, but make no mistake: we are not fighting to be righteous. We already are righteous. We are simply learning to live outwardly like the person we are inwardly.

In the passage that I quoted from Colossians, Paul says we are to strip off our old nature and put on a new nature. In other words, stop acting like who we are not and instead act like who we are.

It is exhausting to act as if we're somebody we are not. Yet that's how we often approach God's commands.

Popular opinion says holiness is hard. Godliness is hard. Giving is hard. Compassion is hard. Winning the lost is hard. But not if it's who I am. All of a sudden, I've just got to be me. That's not so hard. I can do that.

Often, we tell ourselves: *All right, you selfish human being, go love somebody for Jesus today.* And we reply to ourselves: *Okay, that's not who I really am, but I'll try. I'll put on a smile, but I don't want to.*

For some reason, we tend to think that "being a Christian" means "being what I'm not." But that's not true.

Jesus gave me a new way to be human. At the core of my being, I am holy, righteous, godly, compassionate, generous, loving, and sensitive. I have a new nature, and it mirrors the God who created me.

We have to stop seeing ourselves as sinners. In heaven there is no concept of us as sinners. As far as the east is from the west, the Bible says, that is how far God has removed our sins from us. He does not remember them. When God sees us, he does not see a sinner. He sees a saint.

This is who we really are.

Really.

I'm not saying that to trick you into feeling better about yourself. It is not a word game we play to justify sin. It is the good news of grace.

Sometimes sin can seem so big and immovable that we think, *This is who I really am. This is the real truth. What I really am is fallen. What I really am is unholy. What I really am is lustful. What I really am is a liar. What I really am is a negative person. It's in my family. It's my nature. It's my tendency.*

So we sin. And we hate it. And we try to fight it, but it's as if we are fighting ourselves.

"Tell 'em that it's human nature. Why? Why?"

No thanks, Michael, not anymore. I don't do things that way anymore. That's not who I am. When I do things that are ungodly, I'm not acting like who I am.

Yes, these sins are real. But they do not define us. Anger, wrath, malice, evil words—this is not who we are. We have to view those things as intrusions. Sin is an alien, an invader, a parasite. It's not part of God's creation.

The real me is the righteous me, and that is more real than sin could ever be.

To save humanity, God became man in the person of Jesus. In the process, he redefined what it means to belong to the human race.

Jesus came to show us a new way to be human.

Conclusion

JESUS IS

My goal in this book has been to help you see Jesus for who he really is and to understand what that means for your life. It is a reflection of a personal journey I have been on for several years now, a journey that has transformed me from the inside out. I am more in love with Jesus than ever before. I am more excited about preaching the gospel than ever before.

My prayer is that the love of Jesus will consume you, that it will permeate your life and bring color to your existence. There is nothing like it.

This is just the beginning. I'm convinced that the love of Jesus and the beauty of grace are so massive, so extraordinary and extravagant, that we will spend a lifetime discovering their implications.

If certain topics in this book have struck a chord with you, I encourage you to respond. That might mean getting connected to a church near you that will help you grow in Jesus.

It might mean slowing down and spending more time letting Jesus love you. It might mean making some changes in your lifestyle.

If I could leave you with one thing, it would be this: don't let anything stop you from getting right with God. No matter what you might have done, no matter who you are, it's never too late for grace.

The Bible says that salvation is a gift. It's free. We don't need to clean up our acts before we approach God. We don't need to make a sacrifice or pay for our sins. We receive forgiveness by faith, which simply means we choose to believe that Jesus died in our place.

I know it sounds too good to be true.

That's why it's called grace.

And that's who Jesus is.

Acknowledgments

Thanks Jesus.

Thanks Chelsea.

Thanks Nuggets (Zion, Eliott, and Grace).

Thanks Dad.

Thanks Mom.

Thanks Family.

Thanks Friends.

Thanks Church.

Thanks Hillsong.

Thanks Thomas Nelson.

Thanks Esther.

Thanks Justin.

Thanks Sean.

Thanks Andrew.

About the Author

Judah and Chelsea Smith are the lead pastors of the City Church in Seattle, Washington. Judah is a well-known speaker at conferences and churches around the world. His humorous yet poignant messages demystify the Bible and show people who Jesus is in their everyday lives.

Prior to assuming the lead pastorate in 2009, Judah led the youth ministry of the City Church for ten years. He has authored several books and is a popular voice on Twitter (@judahsmith).

Judah and Chelsea have three children: Zion, Eliott, and Grace. Judah is an avid golfer and all-around sports fan. He believes the Seahawks are God's favorite team and is praying for the Sonics to come back to Seattle.

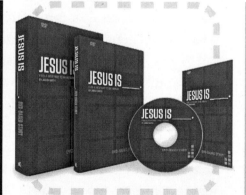